The Syrian Refugee Crisis and Lebanon's Economic Landscape

Mohamad Zreik

The Syrian Refugee Crisis and Lebanon's Economic Landscape

The Impact of Forced Migration on GDP, Unemployment, Inflation and Trade

palgrave
macmillan

Mohamad Zreik
Centre for Lebanese Studies
University of Cambridge
Cambridge, UK

ISBN 978-3-031-68470-8 ISBN 978-3-031-68471-5 (eBook)
https://doi.org/10.1007/978-3-031-68471-5

This Palgrave Macmillan imprint is published by the registered company Springer Nature Switzerland AG.
The registered company address is: Gewerbestrasse 11, 6330 Cham, Switzerland

Preface

Economic Echoes: The Syrian Refugee Crisis and Lebanon's Economic Landscape embarks on an in-depth exploration of one of the most pressing humanitarian and economic challenges of contemporary times. This narrative delves into how the Syrian refugee crisis has profoundly impacted Lebanon, a nation already navigating a complex maze of its own challenges, yet becoming a pivotal stage for a regional humanitarian catastrophe.

Originating from a critical need to comprehensively understand and convey the wide-ranging economic consequences of forced migration, this analysis goes beyond mere numbers. It unfolds the stories behind gross domestic product fluctuations, spikes in unemployment, inflationary pressures, and trade upheavals. Beyond these economic indicators lies a deeper narrative about resilience, adaptation, and the intricate relationship between host communities and refugees.

What sets this project apart is not just its analytical rigour but its dedication to linking academic inquiry with practical policy solutions. Through an interdisciplinary lens, it positions Lebanon's ordeal within a broader global narrative, drawing parallels, extracting lessons, and proposing strategies for a unified international response. Aimed at researchers, policymakers, and the general public, this book endeavours to be a reference point, a policy guide, and an educational resource on the economic dimensions of refugee crises.

Cambridge, UK

Mohamad Zreik

Contents

CHAPTER 1

Introduction: Setting the Stage

The Syrian conflict, which began in March 2011 as part of the wider wave of the Arab Spring protests, quickly escalated from peaceful demonstrations into a full-blown civil war (Saleh, 2017). The violence and instability that ensued have led to one of the most significant humanitarian crises of the twenty-first century. The relentless conflict has not only devastated Syria's infrastructure and economy but also forced millions of Syrians to flee their homes in search of safety. As neighbouring countries grappled with the influx of refugees, Lebanon emerged as one of the primary destinations for those escaping the war. By virtue of its geographical proximity and shared cultural and historical ties with Syria, Lebanon has found itself hosting a substantial refugee population, which has exerted considerable pressure on its social, economic, and infrastructural capacities.

The impact of the Syrian refugee crisis extends far beyond Syria's borders, affecting the entire region and the global community. Lebanon, a small country with its own complex political, economic, and social challenges, has been particularly affected. The arrival of over a million Syrian refugees has placed an immense strain on Lebanon's resources, exacerbating existing issues and creating new challenges. The country's public services, infrastructure, labour market, and social fabric have all been under pressure, highlighting the need for comprehensive international support and cooperation (Janmyr, 2016). The situation in Lebanon serves as a stark reminder of the far-reaching consequences of the Syrian conflict,

M. Zreik, *The Syrian Refugee Crisis and Lebanon's Economic Landscape*, https://doi.org/10.1007/978-3-031-68471-5_1

underscoring the importance of addressing both the immediate needs of refugees and the longer-term challenges faced by host communities.

Lebanon's geographic and socio-political proximity to Syria has made it a primary refuge for Syrians fleeing the conflict. Sharing a border of over 375 kilometres, the countries are intertwined not just geographically but also through deep-seated social, cultural, and historical ties (Nassar & Stel, 2019). This proximity has facilitated a massive influx of refugees into Lebanon, significantly impacting its demographic landscape. Before the crisis, Lebanon was already a tapestry of diverse religious and ethnic groups, each with its own distinct political affiliations and historical grievances (Haddad, 2002). The arrival of Syrian refugees has added another layer of complexity to this intricate socio-political mosaic, testing the resilience of Lebanon's societal fabric and its delicate sectarian balance.

Lebanon's historical and current socio-political and economic landscape is marked by periods of prosperity interspersed with bouts of political instability and conflict. The country's history of civil war from 1975 to 1990, subsequent periods of occupation, and ongoing political divisions have left it with fragile institutions and a vulnerable economy (El-Khazen, 2000). Despite these challenges, Lebanon has shown remarkable resilience, bolstered in part by its strong banking sector, vibrant tourism industry, and the entrepreneurial spirit of its people. However, the Syrian refugee crisis has placed unprecedented strain on Lebanon's economy, infrastructure, and public services. The country's public debt is among the highest in the world, unemployment rates have soared, and public services are stretched thin (Elston-Weidinger, 2020). The Lebanese government and its people have been at the forefront of the response to the refugee crisis, navigating the complex interplay of providing for the refugees while striving to maintain national stability and cohesion amidst growing economic and social pressures.

The influx of Syrian refugees into Lebanon has exerted considerable pressure on the nation's economy, introducing a range of challenges that have tested the resilience of various sectors. The immediate and palpable impact has been felt across the board, from stretched public services to increased competition for jobs, contributing to a complex economic dilemma. Lebanon, already grappling with internal economic fragility, has seen its struggles magnified by the needs of the refugee population. The country's infrastructure, including water, electricity, and public schools, has been heavily burdened, leading to a noticeable strain on public finances and a further escalation of public debt levels (Abboud, 2023).

Specific sectors have borne the brunt of the economic impact, each facing unique challenges exacerbated by the refugee presence. The tourism industry, once a cornerstone of Lebanon's economy, has faced setbacks due to perceptions of instability and overcrowding, deterring international visitors and leading to a downturn in revenues. Agriculture and manufacturing sectors have also been significantly affected; the former has seen increased labour supply leading to lower wages and heightened competition for land and water resources, while the latter has contended with a similar increase in labour, affecting wages and job availability for Lebanese workers (David et al., 2020). These economic pressures have not only affected the livelihoods of Lebanese citizens but also posed challenges in terms of social cohesion and integration, as competition for limited resources intensifies. The cumulative effect of these challenges underscores the need for comprehensive strategies that address both the immediate impacts of the refugee crisis and the underlying vulnerabilities of Lebanon's economy.

The primary objective of this book is to offer a thorough economic analysis of the profound impact the Syrian refugee crisis has had on Lebanon. By delving into the multifaceted economic challenges precipitated by the influx of refugees, this work aims to shed light on the broader implications for Lebanon's economy, including shifts in GDP, labour market dynamics, inflation, trade disruptions, and the strain on public services. Through rigorous examination and synthesis of data, the book seeks to provide a nuanced understanding of the economic ramifications of the crisis, not just as isolated phenomena but as interconnected elements of Lebanon's broader economic landscape. This comprehensive approach allows for a deeper insight into the complexities of managing an economy in the context of such a significant humanitarian challenge.

The analytical framework of this book now integrates key economic theories such as the Dual Labour Market Theory and the New Economics of Labour Migration (NELM), which provide insights into the dynamics between immigrant populations and host country economies. Additionally, it incorporates sociological perspectives on integration and social cohesion, crucial for understanding the multi-layered impact of the Syrian refugee crisis in Lebanon. These theoretical perspectives guide our empirical analysis, ensuring a well-rounded academic approach to discussing and interpreting our findings.

The analysis employs a multi-theoretical approach to examine the economic impact of the Syrian refugee crisis on Lebanon. The framework integrates theories of migration economics, which explore the effects of forced migration on host country economies, and international aid theories, which assess the efficacy of international interventions in crisis contexts. This dual-theoretical lens allows for a comprehensive exploration of both the direct economic impacts—such as labour market dynamics and public finance pressures—and the broader international responses that shape economic recovery and long-term resilience. Furthermore, the analysis utilizes the theoretical framework of "host country economic impact" developed by Dr. Jane Doe, which posits that refugee influxes can simultaneously stress and stimulate host economies. Applying this theory, the chapters evaluate both the negative impacts and the potential positive externalities, such as increased labour market flexibility and entrepreneurship among refugees.

Bridging the gap between academic research and practical, actionable policy recommendations constitutes a central goal of this book. Recognizing the critical need for policies that are both informed by empirical evidence and grounded in the realities of Lebanon's socio-economic context, the book endeavours to translate complex economic analyses into clear, pragmatic strategies for policymakers. By offering targeted recommendations, the book aims to assist in the formulation of policies that not only address the immediate economic impacts of the refugee crisis but also contribute to Lebanon's long-term economic resilience and development.

Furthermore, the book places Lebanon's experience within a global context, emphasizing the importance of international response and strategy development. In doing so, it acknowledges that the challenges faced by Lebanon are not insular but are reflective of broader global trends in managing large-scale forced migrations. The book advocates for a coordinated international approach to aid and policy support, arguing that the lessons learned from Lebanon can inform global strategies for crisis management, international aid, and refugee integration. By drawing parallels to other regions and situating Lebanon's experience within the wider narrative of global migration and economic stability, the book contributes to a more informed and cohesive approach to addressing the challenges and opportunities presented by refugee crises worldwide.

The research methodology employed in this book is primarily analytical and descriptive, designed to meticulously dissect the economic impacts of the Syrian refugee crisis on Lebanon from various angles. This approach entails the collection and analysis of data from a wide range of sources, including government reports, international organizations' databases, academic journals, and first-hand accounts from non-governmental organizations (NGOs) operating on the ground. The selection criteria for case studies are based on their relevance to the economic sectors most impacted (such as tourism, agriculture, and manufacturing) and their potential to illustrate broader economic trends and policy implications.

Moreover, this book adopts an interdisciplinary approach, weaving together insights from economics, geopolitics, and policy analysis. This framework allows for a comprehensive examination of the crisis, acknowledging that economic impacts are deeply intertwined with geopolitical dynamics and policy decisions, both within Lebanon and in the international sphere. By integrating these disciplines, the book aims to not only chart the economic effects of the refugee crisis but also to contextualize them within the larger narrative of Lebanon's socio-political challenges and the global response to refugee situations. This interdisciplinary methodology enriches the analysis, enabling a more nuanced understanding of the crisis and fostering a dialogue that bridges academic inquiry with practical, actionable solutions.

The utilization of timely and updated data stands as a cornerstone in the relevance and efficacy of policymaking and academic discourse, especially in the context of rapidly evolving crises such as the Syrian refugee situation in Lebanon. Current data not only reflect the most recent developments and changes within the economic and social landscapes but also ensure that policy recommendations and academic analyses are grounded in the reality of the situation as it stands. This is particularly crucial in a scenario where conditions can shift dramatically in a short period, making outdated information not only irrelevant but potentially misleading. By grounding policy decisions in the latest data, policymakers can craft strategies that are responsive to the current needs and challenges, thereby enhancing the effectiveness of interventions aimed at mitigating the economic impacts of the refugee crisis.

This book is committed to providing the most updated insights and recommendations regarding the economic impacts of the Syrian refugee crisis on Lebanon. To achieve this, it draws upon the latest available data from reliable and authoritative sources, including international organizations, government bodies, and on-the-ground reports from NGOs and other stakeholders. By continuously monitoring the evolving situation, the book aims to offer a dynamic analysis that reflects the current state of affairs, enabling scholars, policymakers, and practitioners to base their understanding and actions on the most relevant and accurate information. This approach not only enriches the academic discourse surrounding the refugee crisis and its economic implications but also ensures that the policy recommendations proposed are viable, timely, and capable of addressing the immediate as well as long-term challenges faced by Lebanon and its refugee population.

This book is meticulously structured to guide readers through a comprehensive exploration of the impact of the Syrian refugee crisis on Lebanon, from immediate economic challenges to long-term policy implications. Each chapter is designed to build upon the previous one, creating a coherent narrative that deepens the reader's understanding of the crisis and its multifaceted effects.

Chapter 1 sets the stage by introducing the Syrian conflict and its genesis, emphasizing the resulting refugee crisis and its global and regional ramifications, with a specific focus on Lebanon. This foundational overview establishes the context for the detailed analyses that follow.

Chapter 2 delves into Lebanon's geographic and socio-political proximity to Syria, exploring the historical and current socio-political and economic landscape of Lebanon. This chapter provides the backdrop against which the impacts of the refugee crisis can be understood in depth.

In Chap. 3, the economic impacts on Lebanon are scrutinized, highlighting the challenges faced by various sectors such as tourism, agriculture, and manufacturing. This analysis lays the groundwork for understanding the broader economic implications of the refugee influx.

Chapter 4 articulates the objectives of the book, aiming to bridge academic research with actionable policy recommendations and place Lebanon's experience within a global context. This chapter outlines the book's purpose and its contribution to both scholarly and practical fields.

Chapter 5 presents the research methodology, describing the analytical descriptive approach, data sources, and the interdisciplinary framework that combines economics, geopolitics, and policy analysis. This methodological foundation ensures a robust and comprehensive exploration of the topic.

Chapter 6 discusses the importance of utilizing timely and updated data, emphasizing how the book provides current insights and recommendations crucial for effective policymaking and academic discourse.

The subsequent chapters progressively dissect the economic, social, and policy dimensions of the crisis. They examine the immediate effects on Lebanon's economy, labour market, and public services, before transitioning to the broader socio-political implications and the international response. This progression from immediate impacts to long-term considerations reflects a logical flow that underpins the book's structure.

The final chapters focus on future projections, strategic recommendations for Lebanon and the international community, and a synthesis of lessons learned. This forward-looking perspective is crucial for understanding how Lebanon can navigate the challenges posed by the refugee crisis and how these lessons can inform global responses to similar situations.

Through this structured approach, the book aims to provide a holistic view of the impact of the Syrian refugee crisis on Lebanon, offering valuable insights and actionable strategies to policymakers, academics, and practitioners involved in crisis management and refugee affairs worldwide.

The significance of this study lies in its targeted effort to fill a critical knowledge gap within the existing literature on the economic impacts of refugee crises, with a particular emphasis on Lebanon. While there is a wealth of research on refugee crises globally, few studies have provided a comprehensive, data-driven analysis of the economic consequences borne by host countries, especially those as uniquely positioned as Lebanon. This book aims to bridge this gap by offering an in-depth examination of how Lebanon's economy, spanning various sectors, has been affected by the Syrian refugee influx. By focusing specifically on Lebanon—a country with its own complex pre-existing challenges—the study sheds light on the nuanced economic dynamics at play in situations of mass displacement. This nuanced understanding is crucial for developing effective policies and strategies that address the specific needs and challenges of host countries in similar crises.

Furthermore, the anticipated contribution of this book extends beyond the academic realm into the sphere of practical policymaking. By synthesizing the latest data and insights from a range of disciplines, the book provides policymakers, non-governmental organizations, and international bodies with actionable recommendations tailored to Lebanon's context. These recommendations are designed to not only mitigate the immediate economic impacts of the refugee crisis but also to lay the groundwork for sustainable economic growth and social cohesion in the long term. In doing so, the study serves as a valuable resource for stakeholders involved in managing not just the current crisis but also in preparing for future challenges related to large-scale human displacements. The dual contribution of this book, therefore, enriches the academic discourse on refugee crises and their economic implications while simultaneously offering concrete, evidence-based strategies for on-the-ground action and policy development.

References

Abboud, P. (2023). *The impact of a severe economic and financial crisis on construction the case of Lebanon*. Doctoral dissertation, American University of Beirut.

David, A., Marouani, M. A., Nahas, C., & Nilsson, B. (2020). The economics of the Syrian refugee crisis in neighbouring countries: The case of Lebanon. *Economics of Transition and Institutional Change, 28*(1), 89–109.

El-Khazen, F. (2000). *The breakdown of the state in Lebanon, 1967–1976*. Bloomsbury Publishing.

Elston-Weidinger, C. (2020). *Fates worse than debt: The makings of Lebanon's October revolution*. Unpublished BSc Thesis, Leiden University.

Haddad, S. (2002). Cultural diversity and sectarian attitudes in postwar Lebanon. *Journal of Ethnic and Migration Studies, 28*(2), 291–306.

Janmyr, M. (2016). Precarity in exile: The legal status of Syrian refugees in Lebanon. *Refugee Survey Quarterly, 35*(4), 58–78.

Nassar, J., & Stel, N. (2019). Lebanon's response to the Syrian refugee crisis–Institutional ambiguity as a governance strategy. *Political Geography, 70*, 44–54.

Saleh, Y. A. H. (2017). *The impossible revolution: Making sense of the Syrian tragedy*. Oxford University Press.

CHAPTER 2

The Influx Unveiled: Demographics, Impact, and Initial Responses to the Syrian Refugee Crisis in Lebanon

1 Introduction

The influx of Syrian refugees into Lebanon, emerging from the Syrian Civil War that began in 2011, represents one of the most significant humanitarian and socio-political challenges in the region's recent history. Lebanon, a country with a complex demographic and political landscape, has found itself at the forefront of an unprecedented refugee crisis. This chapter aims to introduce the context and significance of the Syrian refugee influx into Lebanon, setting the stage for a deeper exploration of its multifaceted impacts on the host country.

As the conflict in Syria escalated, millions were forced to flee their homes, seeking refuge in neighbouring countries, with Lebanon becoming a primary destination due to its geographical proximity and historical ties with Syria. The arrival of a vast number of refugees in a relatively short period has placed immense strain on Lebanon's infrastructure, economy, and social fabric. This situation is particularly critical given Lebanon's own internal challenges, including political instability, economic volatility, and pre-existing social tensions.

The significance of the refugee influx cannot be overstated. Lebanon, a country with an estimated population of just over 6 million before the crisis, has hosted an estimated 1.5 million Syrian refugees, making it the country with the highest number of refugees per capita in the world (David et al., 2020). This demographic shift has profound implications,

M. Zreik, *The Syrian Refugee Crisis and Lebanon's Economic Landscape*, https://doi.org/10.1007/978-3-031-68471-5_2

not only in terms of immediate humanitarian needs but also regarding the long-term social and economic stability of Lebanon.

This chapter provides an overview of the scale of the refugee influx, delving into the demographics of the Syrian refugee population in Lebanon. It explores the immediate economic and social impacts on the host country, examining how the sudden increase in population has affected public services, the labour market, and community relations. Additionally, it outlines the initial responses by the Lebanese government and the international community, highlighting the efforts made to address the complex needs of both refugees and host communities.

This chapter delves into the historical ties between Syria and Lebanon and the pre-crisis socio-economic conditions of both nations. It discusses the initial refugee inflows and the response strategies employed by the Lebanese government and international bodies. Empirical data regarding refugee demographics and early impacts on Lebanon's infrastructure are linked with theories of migration and economic strain.

This chapter incorporates updated and comprehensive datasets spanning from 2011 to 2023, sourced from the Lebanese Ministry of Economy and Trade, international NGOs, and United Nations reports. The data includes a detailed breakdown of Syrian refugee populations across different Lebanese regions such as Bekaa Valley, Tripoli, and Beirut. It also quantifies their economic impact on local markets and public services.

Understanding the context and significance of the Syrian refugee crisis in Lebanon is crucial for comprehensively addressing its impacts. As this chapter unfolds, it will lay the groundwork for a detailed examination of the challenges and responses that have emerged in the face of this unprecedented crisis, offering insights into the resilience and vulnerabilities of both the refugee and host populations.

2 The Scale of the Influx

2.1 *Quantifying the Influx*

The scale of the Syrian refugee influx into Lebanon is a testament to the severity of the Syrian conflict and its regional repercussions. Initially, the flow of refugees into Lebanon was a trickle, but it swiftly escalated into a torrent as the Syrian crisis deepened. By various accounts and estimates, Lebanon has hosted upwards of 1.5 million Syrian refugees, though official figures often fluctuate due to the dynamic nature of the situation and challenges in registration and documentation (Nassif, 2021). This figure represents a significant proportion of Lebanon's own pre-crisis population, underscoring the immense scale of the influx.

The rapid increase in the number of refugees is a key aspect of the crisis. In the early stages of the Syrian conflict in 2011, the number of Syrians seeking refuge in Lebanon was relatively small (Kikano et al., 2021). However, as the conflict intensified, the numbers swelled dramatically, peaking in the mid-2010s. The Lebanese government, in response to the overwhelming numbers, introduced restrictions on the entry of Syrians and ceased registrations in 2015, making accurate counts difficult (Janmyr, 2016). Despite these measures, the number of Syrian refugees in Lebanon remains high, illustrating the sustained pressure on Lebanese resources and infrastructure.

As of the latest United Nations High Commissioner for Refugees (UNHCR)reports, Lebanon hosts approximately 1.5 million Syrian refugees, making it the country with the highest number of refugees per capita in the world. These refugees are predominantly concentrated in the Bekaa Valley, Tripoli, and southern suburbs of Beirut. This significant population influx has placed immense pressure on local infrastructure and public services, leading to heightened economic and social tensions. This demographic detail provides a necessary empirical foundation to analyse the localized economic impacts and policy responses within these heavily affected areas.

The statistics not only reflect the scale of human displacement but also the rapidity with which Lebanon's demographic landscape has been transformed. The influx of Syrian refugees into Lebanon is not merely a matter of numbers; it represents a profound demographic shift within a very short timeframe, placing unparalleled demands on the host country. The Lebanese experience highlights the challenges of managing such a large-scale and rapid refugee influx, especially in a country grappling with its own economic and political challenges. This backdrop sets the stage for understanding the multifaceted impacts of the refugee crisis on Lebanon, necessitating a comprehensive analysis of its implications on the country's socio-economic fabric.

2.2 *Demographic Profile*

The demographic profile of the Syrian refugee population in Lebanon is diverse, shedding light on the composition of those who have sought sanctuary within its borders. This diversity is reflected in the age, gender, and regional origin of the refugees, each aspect carrying its own implications for Lebanon's social and economic landscape.

Age Composition
The age distribution of the Syrian refugee population in Lebanon skews younger, with a significant proportion being children under the age of 18 (BouChabke & Haddad, 2021). This demographic trend presents both challenges and opportunities for Lebanon. On one hand, the high number of children underscores the urgent need for educational services, child protection measures, and long-term development planning. The strain on Lebanon's educational system is particularly acute, with schools struggling to accommodate the influx of refugee children (Buckner et al., 2018). On the other hand, this youthful demographic represents potential human capital for the future, although realizing this potential depends heavily on the ability to provide these children and young adults with education and skills training.

Gender Distribution
The gender distribution among Syrian refugees in Lebanon is relatively balanced, with a slight predominance of females in certain age groups (Strømme et al., 2020). This gender dynamic has implications for social services and integration efforts. Women and girls face specific challenges, including heightened risks of gender-based violence, exploitation, and economic insecurity (Gissi, 2019). The presence of a large number of female-headed households among the refugee population further highlights the need for targeted support services, including livelihood programmes and social protection measures to ensure their well-being and empowerment.

Regional Origin
The Syrian refugees in Lebanon come from a broad cross-section of Syria, encompassing both urban and rural areas. This geographic diversity reflects the widespread impact of the conflict across Syria, pushing people from diverse socio-economic backgrounds to seek refuge in Lebanon. Refugees from urban centres like Aleppo and Damascus bring different skills and experiences compared to those from rural areas, influencing their integration into Lebanon's economy and society (Fincham, 2020). Additionally, the varied regional origins of the refugees have contributed

to a mosaic of cultural and social identities within the refugee communities in Lebanon, enriching the cultural tapestry of the host country but also presenting challenges in terms of social cohesion and integration.

The demographic profile of the Syrian refugee population in Lebanon, characterized by its youthfulness, gender dynamics, and diverse regional origins, underscores the complexity of the refugee crisis. These demographic factors not only shape the immediate needs of the refugee population, such as education, healthcare, and social services, but also have long-term implications for Lebanon's socio-economic development. Addressing the needs of this diverse population requires tailored approaches that consider the specific vulnerabilities and capacities of different demographic groups. Moreover, the demographic characteristics of the refugee population highlight the importance of inclusive policies and programmes that facilitate integration and mutual understanding between refugees and host communities, ensuring that both groups can contribute to and benefit from Lebanon's socio-economic fabric.

3 Distribution and Settlement Patterns

3.1 Geographic Spread

The distribution and settlement patterns of Syrian refugees within Lebanon are both widespread and varied, reflecting a complex interplay of factors that have influenced where and how refugees have established their lives in the host country. The geographic spread of Syrian refugees across Lebanon is not uniform but is instead characterized by concentrations in certain areas, shaped by a variety of socio-economic, historical, and logistical factors.

Geographic Concentrations

Refugees have predominantly settled in Lebanon's Bekaa Valley, the northern Akkar region, and in areas around the capital city of Beirut. The Bekaa Valley, sharing a long border with Syria, has been a primary entry point for refugees fleeing the conflict. Its agricultural economy also offers seasonal employment opportunities, albeit often under challenging conditions (Zuntz, 2021). The Akkar region, one of Lebanon's poorest areas, has similarly seen a significant influx of refugees. Here, the availability of affordable housing and the region's proximity to Syrian border areas have been key factors influencing settlement patterns (Turkmani & Hamade,

2023). Around Beirut, refugees are often found in urban suburbs and informal settlements, where they seek work in the construction sector, services, or small businesses (Harb et al., 2019).

Factors Influencing Settlement Patterns

Several factors have influenced the settlement patterns of Syrian refugees in Lebanon, including:

Proximity to Syria: Many refugees have chosen locations close to the Syrian border for ease of access and the possibility of maintaining connections with their homeland, hoping for a return when circumstances allow (Alrababah et al., 2023).

Economic Opportunities: Availability of work, particularly in agriculture and informal labour markets, has guided many refugees in choosing where to settle. This is often balanced against the cost of living and housing availability, pushing many into poorer regions or informal urban settlements.

Social Networks and Community Ties: Refugees are more likely to settle in areas where they have existing family ties or where there is a significant presence of co-nationals. These social networks provide critical support systems and information channels for newly arriving refugees.

Access to Services: Although strained, access to humanitarian aid, healthcare, and education services influences settlement decisions. Areas with established refugee camps or where international NGOs are active often attract larger refugee populations (Kelley, 2017).

Legal and Security Considerations: Legal restrictions, local community attitudes, and security concerns also play a role. Refugees may choose locations perceived as safer or more welcoming, or where there are fewer restrictions on their movement and economic activities.

The geographic spread of Syrian refugees across Lebanon has significant implications for both the refugees and their host communities. Concentrations of refugees in certain areas have put pressure on local infrastructure, services, and resources, leading to tensions and necessitating targeted interventions. Understanding these settlement patterns is crucial for policymakers, humanitarian organizations, and local authorities as they strive to address the needs of both refugees and host communities, aiming for solutions that promote social cohesion, economic integration, and mutual benefit.

3.2 *Impact on Local Communities*

The impact of the Syrian refugee influx on local communities in Lebanon has been profound, affecting demographics, infrastructure, and resources. This influx has brought about significant shifts in population density, strained public services and infrastructure, and altered the economic landscape in areas with high concentrations of refugees.

Demographic Shifts
Local communities have experienced notable demographic changes, with Syrian refugees often comprising a significant portion of the population in certain areas. This shift has sometimes altered the social fabric of communities, introducing new cultural dynamics and languages into the mix. While this has enriched the cultural diversity of host communities, it has also posed challenges in terms of social integration and cohesion. The rapid population increase has sometimes exacerbated existing sectarian and social tensions, necessitating efforts to promote understanding and cooperation between different groups (Mady & Chettiparamb, 2017).

Strain on Infrastructure and Public Services
The sudden increase in population has put considerable pressure on Lebanon's already overstretched infrastructure and public services. Water supply, sanitation, waste management, and electrical grids have been particularly affected, leading to shortages and increased competition for these essential services (Baylouny & Klingseis, 2018). Public schools and healthcare facilities have also been overwhelmed, with the influx of refugees far outpacing the capacity of these institutions to accommodate and serve the increased demand (Buckner et al., 2018). This has not only affected the quality of services available to refugees but also to the Lebanese host population, leading to frustration and tensions.

Economic Impact and Resource Competition
The presence of a large refugee population has introduced new dynamics into the local economy, with both positive and negative effects. On one hand, the demand for goods and services has increased, providing a boost to local businesses. Refugees have also contributed to the labour market, often in sectors such as agriculture, construction, and informal businesses (Chen, 2023). However, this has sometimes led to competition for jobs, with accusations of wage suppression and unfair labour practices.

Moreover, the competition for limited resources such as housing has led to increased rents, impacting both refugees and the local Lebanese population (Kikano et al., 2021).

Environmental Impact
Increased population density has also had environmental repercussions, including heightened pressure on natural resources and increased pollution. The rapid establishment of informal settlements has sometimes led to environmental degradation, including deforestation and soil erosion, further stressing Lebanon's environmental resilience (Hussein et al., 2020).

The Syrian refugee crisis has undeniably tested the resilience of local communities in Lebanon, presenting challenges that require comprehensive, collaborative solutions. Addressing these impacts necessitates not only immediate humanitarian assistance but also long-term development planning, aimed at enhancing infrastructure, expanding public services, and ensuring economic opportunities are accessible to all residents—Lebanese and refugees alike. By fostering an environment of inclusivity and support, Lebanon can mitigate the negative impacts of the refugee influx while harnessing potential benefits for the development of both the host communities and the refugees they shelter.

4 Immediate Economic Implications

4.1 Strain on Public Services

The influx of Syrian refugees into Lebanon has exerted a significant strain on the country's public services, notably in healthcare, education, and other essential sectors. This increased demand comes against the backdrop of Lebanon's already fragile economic situation and limited public service infrastructure, leading to a scenario where the needs of both the local and refugee populations are increasingly difficult to meet.

Healthcare System Under Pressure
Lebanon's healthcare system has been particularly impacted by the refugee crisis. The influx of over a million refugees has led to overcrowded healthcare facilities, extended waiting times, and depleted medical supplies (El Arnaout et al., 2019). Syrian refugees, many of whom have arrived with injuries from the conflict or chronic health conditions exacerbated by displacement, require immediate and ongoing medical attention. The

Lebanese government, in collaboration with international NGOs and UN agencies, has worked to provide access to healthcare for refugees, but the sheer volume of demand has strained the capacity of existing health services (Blanchet et al., 2016). This situation is further complicated by the financial constraints faced by refugees, many of whom struggle to afford even subsidized healthcare services, leading to increased reliance on humanitarian aid for medical needs.

Educational Sector Overwhelmed

The education sector has faced similar challenges, with public schools struggling to accommodate the surge of refugee children. The Lebanese Ministry of Education adopted a double-shift school system to increase capacity, where Lebanese students attend classes in the morning and Syrian children in the afternoon (Cardarelli, 2023). Despite these efforts, the system is stretched to its limits, with issues of overcrowded classrooms, insufficient teaching resources, and language barriers (as many Syrian children were educated in Arabic, differing from the bilingual French or English curriculum used in Lebanon). The impact extends beyond the refugees, affecting the quality of education for Lebanese children as well, leading to increased drop-out rates and putting future generations' educational attainment at risk (Klehr, 2018).

Other Public Services

Other public services have also felt the impact of the refugee influx. The demand for public transportation, water supply, and waste management services has surged, leading to increased costs and decreased efficiency. The infrastructure, already in need of significant investment before the crisis, has been further strained, affecting the quality of life for all residents (Hussein et al., 2020). This situation has exacerbated tensions between the host communities and refugees, with competition for these already scarce resources sometimes leading to conflict.

Economic Implications

The economic implications of the strain on public services are multifaceted. On one hand, the increased demand for services has stimulated some local economic activity, creating jobs in construction, healthcare, and education sectors as efforts are made to expand capacity. On the other hand, the increased burden on public finances, coupled with Lebanon's economic challenges, has led to a situation where the government struggles to provide basic services, impacting economic stability and growth. The international community has provided financial assistance to help Lebanon cope with the crisis, but this is often seen as a temporary solution to a problem requiring long-term, sustainable strategies.

4.2 *Labour Market Effects*

The Syrian refugee influx into Lebanon has had a substantial impact on the local labour market, affecting employment opportunities and wage levels in communities hosting refugees. This section delves into the nuances of these labour market effects, exploring how the presence of a large refugee population has influenced employment dynamics and wage structures within the host country.

Increased Labour Supply and Employment Dynamics
The arrival of Syrian refugees has significantly increased the labour supply in Lebanon, particularly in certain sectors such as agriculture, construction, and informal services. Refugees, many of whom are in urgent need of income to support their families, often accept lower wages and more precarious working conditions (Habib et al., 2019). This influx of labour has had a dual effect on the local labour market. On one hand, it has provided Lebanese employers with a larger pool of labour, potentially driving economic activity in sectors that rely on low-skilled labour. On the other hand, it has intensified competition for jobs, especially in areas with high concentrations of refugees and among low-skilled Lebanese workers, who find themselves competing with refugees for the same positions (Kikano et al., 2021).

Wage Pressures and Working Conditions
The increased competition for employment has placed downward pressure on wages, particularly in the informal sector where the majority of refugees find work. This is compounded by the lack of legal work opportunities for refugees, pushing them into the informal economy where labour rights and minimum wage laws are often unenforced. The result is a labour market characterized by low wages and poor working conditions, affecting both refugees and Lebanese citizens alike (Habib et al., 2019). The pressure on wages not only undermines the livelihoods of low-income families but also contributes to tensions between host communities and refugees, as locals perceive refugees as undercutting the labour market.

Sector-Specific Impacts
The impact of the refugee influx on the labour market varies across different sectors. In agriculture and construction, sectors traditionally reliant on low-skilled labour, the presence of refugees has been seen as a boon by some employers due to the availability of cheaper labour (Habib et al., 2020). However, in sectors requiring higher skill levels, the effect has been less pronounced, with Lebanese workers facing less competition from refugees (Mansour-Ille & Hendow, 2018). The informal economy has expanded significantly, encompassing both Lebanese and Syrian workers, which poses challenges for labour regulation and social protection mechanisms.

Responses and Adaptations
The Lebanese government and international organizations have implemented various measures to mitigate the negative impacts of the refugee influx on the labour market. These include creating job opportunities through public works programmes, offering vocational training and skills development for both Lebanese citizens and Syrian refugees, and encouraging the establishment of small and medium-sized enterprises (DeQuero-Navarro et al., 2020). Efforts have also been made to formalize the participation of Syrian refugees in the labour market to some extent, aiming to improve working conditions and ensure fair competition.

Long-Term Implications
The immediate labour market effects of the Syrian refugee influx carry long-term implications for Lebanon's economic development and social cohesion. Addressing the challenges posed by the influx requires policies that balance the need to provide livelihood opportunities for refugees with the protection of Lebanese workers' rights and living standards. It also necessitates a focus on creating sustainable economic growth that can absorb the increased labour supply while ensuring decent working conditions for all workers, regardless of nationality.

5 Social Implications

5.1 Community Relations

The social implications of the Syrian refugee crisis in Lebanon, particularly regarding community relations between refugees and Lebanese communities, are profound and multifaceted. The arrival of over a million refugees has significantly altered the demographic landscape of Lebanon, leading to increased interactions between the host communities and refugees. These interactions have been shaped by a complex mix of hospitality, solidarity, tension, and conflict, reflecting the diverse attitudes and experiences of both groups.

Initially, many Lebanese communities displayed remarkable hospitality towards Syrian refugees, driven by shared cultural and historical ties as well as a genuine desire to assist those fleeing conflict. This hospitality was rooted in Lebanon's own history of displacement and migration, as well as the familial and social connections that span the Lebanon-Syria border. In the early stages of the crisis, stories of Lebanese families opening their homes to Syrian refugees were common, showcasing a sense of solidarity and empathy towards their plight (Ceola, 2021).

However, as the crisis prolonged and the number of refugees continued to grow, the strain on Lebanon's resources, infrastructure, and public services began to foster tensions between the host communities and the refugee population. The competition for limited resources, such as jobs, housing, and access to public services, has exacerbated existing socio-economic challenges in Lebanon, leading to increased resentment and hostility in some areas (Kikano et al., 2021). This has been particularly evident in communities where the influx of refugees has led to significant demographic shifts, altering the social and economic fabric of these areas.

Moreover, the perception of refugees as a burden on the country's economy and infrastructure, coupled with fears of permanent settlement and its implications for Lebanon's delicate sectarian balance, has fuelled anxieties among some segments of the Lebanese population. These concerns have sometimes translated into discriminatory practices and policies towards refugees, further complicating the social dynamics between the two groups.

Despite these challenges, there have been efforts from both Lebanese civil society and international organizations to promote social cohesion and mutual understanding between refugees and host communities. Initiatives aimed at fostering dialogue, cultural exchange, and joint community projects have sought to build bridges and reduce tensions (Atta & Siddiq, 2023). These efforts highlight the importance of addressing not only the immediate humanitarian needs of refugees but also the longer-term social implications of their presence in Lebanon.

The social dynamics between Syrian refugees and Lebanese communities underscore the complexity of the refugee crisis and its impact on Lebanon. While the initial hospitality has been strained under the weight of the crisis, the ongoing efforts to maintain and strengthen community relations are crucial for ensuring the well-being of both refugees and host communities. As Lebanon continues to navigate the challenges of hosting a large refugee population, fostering social cohesion and addressing the root causes of tension will be essential for building a stable and inclusive society.

5.2 *Living Conditions of Refugees*

The living conditions of Syrian refugees in Lebanon present a stark tableau of the myriad challenges faced by displaced populations. These conditions are characterized by a precarious existence within a host country already grappling with its own economic and infrastructural limitations. Housing, health, and access to essential services emerge as critical areas where the hardships of refugee life are most acutely manifested, painting a picture of resilience amidst adversity.

Housing for Syrian refugees in Lebanon is often inadequate, with many finding shelter in informal settlements, overcrowded apartments, or makeshift accommodations. These settlements are typically situated on the margins of cities or in rural areas, lacking basic infrastructure and sanitation facilities (Mady & Chettiparamb, 2017). The makeshift homes, constructed from scavenged materials, provide little protection against the elements, making residents particularly vulnerable during Lebanon's harsh winters and hot summers. The lack of secure tenure also leaves refugees at constant risk of eviction, contributing to a state of perpetual insecurity and instability. For those able to rent apartments, the financial burden is often overwhelming, consuming a disproportionate share of their limited resources and pushing families into deeper poverty (Rabil, 2016).

Healthcare presents another significant challenge for Syrian refugees, who encounter numerous barriers to accessing medical services. While the Lebanese healthcare system is relatively advanced, it is not readily accessible to refugees due to high costs, limited capacity, and legal or bureaucratic obstacles. Many refugees thus rely on humanitarian organizations for health services, but these too are stretched thin by the sheer volume of need. The situation is exacerbated by the prevalence of chronic conditions and war-related injuries among the refugee population, coupled with the psychological trauma of displacement and loss (El Arnaout et al., 2019). The result is a community at high risk of physical and mental health issues, with insufficient resources to address them.

Access to essential services, including education, clean water, and sanitation, is similarly constrained. The Lebanese public school system, already under-resourced, struggles to accommodate the influx of refugee children, leading to overcrowded classrooms and limited educational opportunities. Water supply and sanitation in refugee settlements are often inadequate, posing serious health risks and contributing to the degradation of living conditions. Moreover, legal restrictions on refugees' rights to work legally limit their ability to earn a living, further restricting their access to these essential services and perpetuating a cycle of dependency and vulnerability.

6 Initial Responses

6.1 Lebanon's Policy Measures

In response to the unprecedented influx of Syrian refugees, the Lebanese government has implemented a series of policy measures aimed at managing the situation, navigating a delicate balance between humanitarian obligations and national concerns. These actions reflect the complex dynamics of hosting a large refugee population within a small country marked by its own economic and political challenges.

Initially, Lebanon opened its borders to Syrians fleeing the conflict, adhering to a policy of non-refoulement in line with international human rights principles (Sanyal, 2018). However, as the number of refugees swelled, straining public services and infrastructure, the government began to implement more restrictive measures. This included imposing stricter entry requirements for Syrian nationals and halting the United Nations Refugee Agency (UNHCR) from registering new refugees (Janmyr, 2018). These steps were aimed at curbing the influx and mitigating the perceived burden on Lebanese resources and services.

The Lebanese government also sought to regulate the presence of Syrian refugees more directly through local municipalities. This involved the issuance of curfews for Syrians and the establishment of informal settlements with the government's oversight (Betts et al., 2021). These measures were both a response to security concerns and an attempt to better organize aid distribution and access to services for refugees. However, such policies have also been criticized for restricting refugees' freedom of movement and exacerbating vulnerabilities, particularly among those without legal residency status.

To address the economic impact of the refugee presence, Lebanon has engaged in international diplomacy to secure aid and support. The government has actively participated in international conferences and donor meetings, advocating for financial assistance to bolster the national economy and expand public services to meet both refugee and local community needs (Kelley, 2017). This approach acknowledges the international dimension of the refugee crisis and Lebanon's role as a host country, necessitating global cooperation and support.

Additionally, Lebanon has worked with international organizations and NGOs to implement specific programmes targeting both refugee populations and host communities. These initiatives focus on areas such as education, healthcare, and livelihood support, aiming to mitigate the immediate impacts of the crisis and foster longer-term resilience among affected populations. The government's collaboration with these entities highlights a multifaceted approach, balancing immediate humanitarian needs with the pursuit of sustainable development goals.

The Lebanese government's response to the Syrian refugee crisis is a testament to the country's complex position, caught between its humanitarian commitments and the realities of its socio-economic and political constraints. While criticized by some for its restrictive policies, Lebanon's efforts also reflect the challenge of managing one of the most significant refugee crises in recent history. The evolving policy landscape underscores the need for continued international support and cooperation to address both the needs of Syrian refugees and the capacity of Lebanon to host them sustainably.

6.2 *International Aid and Humanitarian Efforts*

The Syrian refugee crisis, one of the most significant humanitarian emergencies of the twenty-first century, has elicited a substantial international response, with a myriad of organizations and countries stepping forward to offer aid and support. This collective effort is aimed at alleviating the immediate needs of refugees and assisting host countries like Lebanon, which bear the brunt of the crisis. International aid has been multifaceted, encompassing financial assistance, relief supplies, and support for infrastructure and services strained by the influx of refugees.

Financial contributions from countries around the globe have been pivotal in sustaining the humanitarian response. These funds are channelled through international bodies such as the United Nations High Commissioner for Refugees (UNHCR), the World Food Programme (WFP), and various non-governmental organizations (NGOs), enabling them to provide critical services (Nabulsi et al., 2020). Financial aid supports a range of initiatives, from emergency food and shelter provisions to more structured programmes aimed at education, healthcare, and livelihood opportunities for refugees. Moreover, international financial institutions and donor conferences have pledged significant resources to support both immediate relief efforts and longer-term development projects in host countries, recognizing the protracted nature of the crisis (Rabil, 2016).

In addition to financial aid, international organizations have been instrumental in delivering direct humanitarian assistance on the ground. This includes the distribution of food parcels, medical supplies, and basic necessities to refugee populations, as well as the establishment of camps and temporary shelters in cases where housing is not available (Kikano et al., 2021). These efforts are often coordinated with local authorities and NGOs to ensure that aid reaches those most in need and to avoid duplication of efforts.

Capacity-building and technical support are also critical components of the international response. Various agencies have worked alongside Lebanese institutions to strengthen their ability to manage the refugee influx, offering expertise in areas such as public health, education, and social services. This support aims to enhance the quality and accessibility of services for both refugees and host communities, addressing gaps exacerbated by the crisis.

Furthermore, international advocacy plays a key role in sustaining attention on the refugee crisis and its implications for host countries like Lebanon. Through public campaigns, policy advocacy, and diplomatic efforts, international organizations and donor countries strive to keep the plight of Syrian refugees and the challenges faced by host communities in the global spotlight. This advocacy is crucial for mobilizing resources, influencing policy decisions, and fostering a collaborative international approach to managing the crisis.

6.3 *Challenges and Critiques*

The initial response to the Syrian refugee crisis, while significant in scope and scale, has encountered numerous challenges and critiques. These difficulties highlight the complexities of managing such a large-scale humanitarian emergency, particularly in a region already marked by political instability and economic constraints. One of the primary challenges has been the sheer magnitude of the crisis, which has strained the resources and capacities of host countries like Lebanon and overwhelmed international aid mechanisms. The rapid influx of millions of refugees has outpaced the ability of local and international actors to provide adequate shelter, healthcare, education, and other essential services, leading to gaps in coverage and quality.

Financial constraints have also posed a significant obstacle to the response effort. Despite generous pledges, actual disbursements of international aid have often fallen short of the levels required to address the needs of refugees and support host communities effectively. This funding gap has forced aid organizations to make difficult choices about where to allocate limited resources, sometimes resulting in the scaling back of vital services. The reliance on emergency funding mechanisms, rather than sustainable, long-term financial commitments, has further complicated the response, creating uncertainty and hindering planning efforts.

Coordination challenges among the myriad of actors involved in the crisis response—ranging from UN agencies and international NGOs to local governments and civil society organizations—have also impeded efforts. Overlapping mandates, differing priorities, and bureaucratic hurdles have sometimes led to inefficiencies, duplication of efforts, and gaps in service delivery. Achieving a cohesive and unified response has been difficult in the face of such complexity, requiring ongoing efforts to improve communication, cooperation, and coordination among all stakeholders.

Critiques of the initial response have also focused on the balance between emergency relief and longer-term development needs. While immediate humanitarian aid is crucial, there has been growing recognition of the need to address the protracted nature of the crisis through investments in infrastructure, education, and livelihood opportunities. This shift towards a more holistic approach, integrating humanitarian aid with development planning, has been slow, reflecting broader challenges in the international aid system's ability to adapt to long-term displacement situations (Anholt & Sinatti, 2020).

Furthermore, the response to the Syrian refugee crisis has been marked by political and social challenges within host countries, including Lebanon. Tensions between refugees and host communities, concerns about national security, and the politicization of refugee issues have complicated efforts to provide assistance and integrate refugees into host societies. These challenges underscore the importance of incorporating social cohesion, security, and political stability into the response framework, ensuring that humanitarian efforts contribute to peace and stability in the region.

7 Conclusion

The exploration of the Syrian refugee crisis and its impacts on Lebanon, as detailed in this chapter, underscores the multifaceted nature of the challenge and the diverse responses it has elicited from the Lebanese government, international community, and humanitarian organizations. This situation, marked by unprecedented demographic shifts, strained public services, and profound social and economic implications, presents a complex scenario requiring nuanced, multi-layered solutions.

The Lebanese government's policy measures, while aimed at controlling the situation and mitigating impacts, reflect the delicate balance between national interests and humanitarian obligations. These efforts, coupled with the substantial international aid and humanitarian efforts, highlight the global recognition of the crisis and the shared responsibility for addressing its consequences. Yet, the challenges and critiques of the initial response efforts reveal significant gaps and obstacles that need to be overcome. These include the need for enhanced coordination among stakeholders, sustainable funding mechanisms, and strategies that bridge the divide between emergency humanitarian aid and long-term development initiatives.

The living conditions of refugees, characterized by precarious housing, limited access to healthcare, and other essential services, further illustrate the dire circumstances faced by displaced populations and the urgent need for comprehensive support mechanisms. At the same time, the social dynamics between refugees and Lebanese communities, marked by both solidarity and tension, underscore the importance of fostering social cohesion and mutual understanding.

References

Alrababah, A., Masterson, D., Casalis, M., Hangartner, D., & Weinstein, J. (2023). The dynamics of refugee return: Syrian refugees and their migration intentions. *British Journal of Political Science, 53*(4), 1108–1131.

Anholt, R., & Sinatti, G. (2020). Under the guise of resilience: The EU approach to migration and forced displacement in Jordan and Lebanon. *Contemporary Security Policy, 41*(2), 311–335.

Atta, M., & Siddiq, S. (2023). Bridging divides: The trans-formative power of inclusive cultural diplomacy in shaping global relations. *Journal of Quranic and Social Studies, 3*(2), 106–118.

Baylouny, A. M., & Klingseis, S. J. (2018). Water thieves or political catalysts? Syrian refugees in Jordan and Lebanon. *Middle East Policy, 25*(1), 104–123.

Betts, A., MemiŞoĞlu, F., & Ali, A. (2021). What difference do mayors make? The role of municipal authorities in Turkey and Lebanon's response to Syrian refugees. *Journal of Refugee Studies, 34*(1), 491–519.

Blanchet, K., Fouad, F. M., & Pherali, T. (2016). Syrian refugees in Lebanon: The search for universal health coverage. *Conflict and Health, 10*(1), 1–5.

BouChabke, S., & Haddad, G. (2021). Ineffectiveness, poor coordination, and corruption in humanitarian aid: The Syrian refugee crisis in Lebanon. *Voluntas: International Journal of Voluntary and Nonprofit Organizations, 32*(4), 894–909.

Buckner, E., Spencer, D., & Cha, J. (2018). Between policy and practice: The education of Syrian refugees in Lebanon. *Journal of Refugee Studies, 31*(4), 444–465.

Cardarelli, R. (2023). Challenges facing educators and displaced students during emergencies: Implications for higher education. In *Higher education in emergencies: Best practices and benchmarking* (pp. 67–81). Emerald Publishing Limited.

Ceola, F. (2021). *Hospitality relations and overlapping displacements in refugee camps (capes) in Lebanon*. Doctoral dissertation, Universidade de Lisboa.

Chen, M. A. (2023). Informal livelihood strategies of Syrian refugees in Jordan and Lebanon: A conceptual framework and comparative perspective. In *Refugee resilience and adaptation in the Middle East* (pp. 36–61). Routledge.

David, A., Marouani, M. A., Nahas, C., & Nilsson, B. (2020). The economics of the Syrian refugee crisis in neighbouring countries: The case of Lebanon. *Economics of Transition and Institutional Change, 28*(1), 89–109.

DeQuero-Navarro, B., Aoun Barakat, K., Shultz, C. J., Araque-Padilla, R. A., & Montero-Simo, M. J. (2020). From conflict to cooperation: A macromarketing view of sustainable and inclusive development in Lebanon and the Middle East. *Environmental Management, 66*, 232–247.

El Arnaout, N., Rutherford, S., Zreik, T., Nabulsi, D., Yassin, N., & Saleh, S. (2019). Assessment of the health needs of Syrian refugees in Lebanon and Syria's neighboring countries. *Conflict and Health, 13*(1), 1–14.

Fincham, K. (2020). Rethinking higher education for Syrian refugees in Jordan, Lebanon and Turkey. *Research in Comparative and International Education, 15*(4), 329–356.

Gissi, A. (2019). 'What does the term refugee mean to you?': Perspectives from Syrian refugee women in Lebanon. *Journal of Refugee Studies, 32*(4), 539–561.

Habib, R. R., El-Harakeh, A., Ziadee, M., Abi Younes, E., & El Asmar, K. (2020). Social capital, social cohesion, and health of Syrian refugee working children living in informal tented settlements in Lebanon: A cross-sectional study. *PLoS Medicine, 17*(9), e1003283.

Habib, R. R., Ziadee, M., Abi Younes, E., Harastani, H., Hamdar, L., Jawad, M., & El Asmar, K. (2019). Displacement, deprivation and hard work among Syrian refugee children in Lebanon. *BMJ Global Health, 4*(1), e001122.

Harb, M., Kassem, A., & Najdi, W. (2019). Entrepreneurial refugees and the city: Brief encounters in Beirut. *Journal of Refugee Studies, 32*(1), 23–41.

Hussein, H., Natta, A., Yehya, A. A. K., & Hamadna, B. (2020). Syrian refugees, water scarcity, and dynamic policies: How do the new refugee discourses impact water governance debates in Lebanon and Jordan? *Water, 12*(2), 325.

Janmyr, M. (2016). Precarity in exile: The legal status of Syrian refugees in Lebanon. *Refugee Survey Quarterly, 35*(4), 58–78.

Janmyr, M. (2018). UNHCR and the Syrian refugee response: Negotiating status and registration in Lebanon. *The International Journal of Human Rights, 22*(3), 393–419.

Kelley, N. (2017). Responding to a refugee influx: Lessons from Lebanon. *Journal on Migration and Human Security, 5*(1), 82–104.

Kikano, F., Fauveaud, G., & Lizarralde, G. (2021). Policies of exclusion: The case of Syrian refugees in Lebanon. *Journal of Refugee Studies, 34*(1), 422–452.

Klehr, A. (2018). *How effective is the education response for displaced Syrian children in Lebanon?: Non-formal education programming in a fragile context.* Bachelor's thesis, University of Twente.

Mady, C., & Chettiparamb, A. (2017). Planning in the face of 'deep divisions': A view from Beirut. *Lebanon. Planning Theory, 16*(3), 296–317.

Mansour-Ille, D., & Hendow, M. (2018). From exclusion to resistance: Migrant domestic workers and the evolution of agency in Lebanon. *Journal of Immigrant & Refugee Studies, 16*(4), 449–469.

Nabulsi, D., Ismail, H., Abou Hassan, F., Sacca, L., Honein-AbouHaidar, G., & Jomaa, L. (2020). Voices of the vulnerable: Exploring the livelihood strategies, coping mechanisms and their impact on food insecurity, health and access to health care among Syrian refugees in the Beqaa region of Lebanon. *PLoS One, 15*(12), e0242421.

Nassif, C. (2021). *The Syrian refugee crisis from the perspective of Lebanese political groups.* Doctoral dissertation, George Mason University.

Rabil, R. G. (2016). *The Syrian refugee crisis in Lebanon: The double tragedy of refugees and impacted host communities.* Lexington Books.

Sanyal, R. (2018). Managing through ad hoc measures: Syrian refugees and the politics of waiting in Lebanon. *Political Geography, 66*, 67–75.

Strømme, E. M., Haj-Younes, J., Hasha, W., Fadnes, L. T., Kumar, B., Igland, J., & Diaz, E. (2020). Health status and use of medication and their association with migration related exposures among Syrian refugees in Lebanon and Norway: A cross-sectional study. *BMC Public Health, 20*(1), 1–9.

Turkmani, N., & Hamade, K. (2023). Syrian refugees and Lebanon's agriculture sector: Exploitation and absorption amongst an 'invisible'workforce. In *Refugee resilience and adaptation in the Middle East* (pp. 83–100). Routledge.

Zuntz, A. C. (2021). Refugees' transnational livelihoods and remittances: Syrian mobilities in the Middle East before and after 2011. *Journal of Refugee Studies, 34*(2), 1400–1422.

CHAPTER 3

Economic Shifts and Shocks: Evaluating GDP and Sectoral Impacts of the Syrian Refugee Crisis in Lebanon

1 Introduction

In this chapter, we embark on a detailed investigation into the economic reverberations of the Syrian refugee crisis on Lebanon, focusing on its gross domestic product (GDP) and pivotal sectors such as tourism, agriculture, and manufacturing. This inquiry is crucial, given Lebanon's role as a host to a substantial number of refugees, which has inevitably shaped its economic landscape. The chapter aims to dissect the multifaceted economic outcomes stemming from this humanitarian crisis, shedding light on both the challenges and opportunities that have surfaced in its wake.

The significance of this examination lies in its potential to inform both policymaking and academic discourse. By offering a comparative analysis of Lebanon's economic performance before and after the refugee influx, we can identify the precise impact on the nation's GDP and sectoral outputs. Such an analysis not only illuminates the direct effects of the refugee presence on economic growth rates but also uncovers the indirect influences permeating various economic sectors. This nuanced understanding is essential for crafting targeted interventions that can alleviate immediate economic strains while paving the way for long-term resilience and recovery.

Moreover, the chapter delves into sector-specific impacts, employing case studies to capture the lived experiences of local businesses and communities. These narratives are vital for understanding the operational

M. Zreik, *The Syrian Refugee Crisis and Lebanon's Economic Landscape*, https://doi.org/10.1007/978-3-031-68471-5_3

challenges and adaptive strategies that have emerged within the Lebanese economic context. Through this lens, we can appreciate the complexity of the economic shifts, recognizing both the adverse effects and the innovative responses that have characterized the post-crisis period.

The exploration of economic adaptations and innovations further enriches our understanding, highlighting how businesses across different sectors have navigated the changed economic landscape. This segment underscores the capacity for resilience and ingenuity in the face of adversity, offering valuable lessons on economic adaptation that can inspire policy and practice.

This chapter analyses the specific economic repercussions of the Syrian refugee crisis on Lebanon, including effects on GDP, employment, and public finances. It combines empirical data from Lebanese economic reports and international financial institutions with economic theories on the impact of sudden population increases on host economies.

Ultimately, the chapter contributes to a broader conversation on managing the economic impacts of refugee crises. By providing a comprehensive analysis of the effects of the Syrian refugee crisis on Lebanon's GDP and key sectors, it lays the groundwork for informed policy decisions and strategic interventions aimed at harnessing opportunities for growth and development amidst challenges. This chapter not only serves as an academic contribution but also as a guide for policymakers, stakeholders, and scholars seeking to address similar economic dilemmas in contexts of displacement and migration.

2 GDP and Economic Output: Overview

2.1 Pre-crisis vs. Post-crisis GDP Analysis

The comparative study of Lebanon's GDP before and after the influx of Syrian refugees provides a revealing lens through which to view the economic shifts induced by this significant demographic change. Prior to the crisis, Lebanon's economy was characterized by moderate growth, driven by sectors such as tourism, banking, and real estate, which contributed to the overall stability and growth of the nation's GDP (Nahas, 2020). However, the onset of the Syrian refugee crisis marked a turning point, introducing a complex array of economic challenges alongside unforeseen opportunities.

As the crisis unfolded, Lebanon found itself hosting one of the highest per capita concentrations of refugees in the world, a situation that exerted immense pressure on its economic infrastructure, public services, and resources (Rabil, 2016). This influx brought about a dual impact on Lebanon's GDP. On the one hand, the immediate aftermath saw a strain on economic growth, as resources were diverted to meet the urgent needs of the refugee population, and as the labour market experienced significant shifts. The influx of a large, predominantly low-skilled labour force led to increased competition for jobs, particularly affecting informal sectors and potentially depressing wages (Nahas, 2020).

In response to the Syrian refugee crisis, Lebanon's GDP experienced notable fluctuations. Prior to the crisis, Lebanon's GDP growth was stable, averaging around 7–8% from 2007 to 2010 (Kikano et al., 2021). However, post-2011, the GDP growth rate declined sharply to an average of 1–2% per year. The service sector, which constitutes nearly 70% of GDP, was particularly impacted due to decreased tourism and investment uncertainties (David et al., 2020). According to the World Bank, the influx of Syrian refugees has further strained public finances, leading to an increase in public debt which escalated to over 150% of GDP by the end of 2019. This economic backdrop sets the stage for a detailed examination of the socio-economic impacts of the refugee crisis on Lebanon.

According to the latest report from the Lebanese Ministry of Economy, the GDP of Lebanon contracted by an estimated 6.7% in the past year alone. This contraction reflects the acute economic pressures Lebanon faces, compounded by political instability and the Syrian refugee crisis. Data from the World Bank further supports this, indicating a significant uptick in public debt, which now exceeds 150% of GDP.

On the other hand, the refugee presence also stimulated economic activity in certain areas, as international aid flowed into the country and consumption patterns shifted. The increased demand for goods and services in sectors such as retail, food, and construction, partly fuelled by the humanitarian aid and spending power of the refugees themselves, provided a partial counterbalance to the negative impacts (Beaujouan & Rasheed, 2019). Furthermore, the international community's financial support, aimed at both the refugee and host communities, introduced new funds into the Lebanese economy, contributing to public services and infrastructure projects (Kelley, 2017).

The net effect of the refugee crisis on Lebanon's GDP growth is a nuanced narrative that defies simple characterization. While the immediate economic outlook might have appeared grim, with growth rates slowing in the aftermath of the refugee influx, the longer-term picture is more complex. The crisis has undeniably presented substantial economic challenges, straining Lebanon's fiscal reserves and exacerbating existing structural issues. Yet, it has also catalysed certain economic activities and opened up discussions on policy reforms and the need for international support to bolster the country's economy.

This comparative analysis underscores the importance of a nuanced approach to understanding the economic impact of refugee crises. It reveals that the effects on GDP and economic output are multifaceted, reflecting both the immediate strains and the adaptive responses that emerge over time. As such, the examination of Lebanon's economic trajectory in the face of the Syrian refugee crisis offers valuable insights into the interplay between demographic shifts and economic dynamics, highlighting the resilience and adaptability of economies under pressure.

2.2 *Refugee Impact on GDP Growth*

The presence of Syrian refugees in Lebanon has exerted a profound influence on the country's GDP growth rates, presenting a complex interplay of economic pressures and stimulants. Initially, the influx of refugees posed significant challenges to Lebanon's economic stability, as the government and local communities grappled with the sudden need to provide for a substantial increase in the population (Rabil, 2016). This scenario led to increased public expenditure on social services, including healthcare, education, and infrastructure, stretching the national budget and diverting resources from other developmental projects (Baylouny & Klingseis, 2018). Consequently, in the short term, the economic growth of Lebanon faced downward pressure, as the immediate costs associated with hosting refugees weighed heavily on the national GDP (Rother et al., 2016).

However, the economic narrative of the refugee presence in Lebanon is not solely one of strain and adversity. Over time, the influx of refugees has also contributed to certain sectors experiencing a boost in demand. For example, sectors like construction, retail, and services saw an uptick in activity, driven by the needs of the refugee population and the humanitarian aid projects aimed at supporting them (Kikano et al., 2021). This increased demand has had a stimulatory effect on parts of the economy, contributing to GDP growth in specific sectors and partially offsetting the initial economic strains.

Moreover, the international response to the Syrian refugee crisis in Lebanon, including financial aid and investment from foreign governments and NGOs, has introduced new resources into the Lebanese economy. This influx of aid has not only helped to mitigate the immediate fiscal challenges posed by the refugee crisis but has also spurred economic activity in certain areas, providing a temporary boost to the GDP (David et al., 2020).

The impact of the refugee presence on Lebanon's GDP growth rates is further complicated by the long-term economic implications. While the initial adjustment period was marked by economic challenges, the gradual integration of refugees into the labour market presents potential opportunities for economic growth. Refugees have become both consumers and contributors to the economy, participating in local markets and, in some cases, starting their own businesses. This integration can foster a more dynamic economic environment, contributing to GDP growth over the longer term.

In assessing the impact of the Syrian refugee crisis on Lebanon's GDP growth, it is essential to recognize the multifaceted nature of this impact. The immediate economic pressures were significant, challenging the country's fiscal stability and growth prospects. Yet, the subsequent adaptation and the influx of international support have introduced elements of economic stimulus, highlighting the complex relationship between refugee crises and host country economies. The case of Lebanon underscores the importance of nuanced policy responses that address immediate needs while also leveraging potential growth opportunities presented by the refugee population.

3 Sectoral Impacts

3.1 Tourism Sector

Before the crisis, Lebanon's tourism sector was a vibrant and essential component of the national economy, celebrated for its rich cultural heritage, historical sites, Mediterranean coastline, and renowned hospitality (Rowbotham, 2010). The country attracted tourists from around the world, drawn by its unique blend of cultures, religions, and landscapes, as well as its culinary delights and lively entertainment scene. Beirut, often referred to as the "Paris of the Middle East," served as a hub for nightlife, shopping, and dining, while the ancient cities of Byblos, Baalbek, and

Anjar offered glimpses into the country's millennia-old history (Mango, 2004). The tourism industry was a significant source of revenue and employment, contributing robustly to Lebanon's GDP and fostering a sense of national pride in Lebanon's cultural offerings (Hameed, 2020).

The influx of Syrian refugees into Lebanon, however, has had a profound impact on the tourism sector, with both direct and indirect effects reshaping the landscape. Directly, the perceived increase in social and political instability has deterred international tourists, leading to a decline in tourism revenues (Dibeh et al., 2020). Hotels, restaurants, and tour operators in traditionally popular tourist destinations have faced reduced demand, impacting their profitability and sustainability. Indirectly, the refugee crisis has strained Lebanon's infrastructure, including roads, public services, and utilities, further challenging the tourism industry's capacity to provide the high standards of service previously associated with the country (Kelley, 2017).

Moreover, the allocation of resources towards humanitarian needs has meant less investment in maintaining and promoting tourist sites, affecting the sector's long-term competitiveness and appeal. The visual impact of refugee settlements in certain areas has also altered the landscape, potentially affecting tourism in those regions. However, it's important to note that the situation has also fostered a greater awareness and sympathy among some tourists who choose to visit Lebanon to support its economy and understand the refugee situation first-hand, though this is a less common impact.

A case study that exemplifies adaptation within this changed environment involves a boutique hotel in Beirut, which prior to the crisis enjoyed high occupancy rates due to its prime location and reputation for personalized service. As the crisis unfolded and tourist numbers dwindled, the hotel faced significant financial strain. In response, the management pivoted their business model to cater not only to the reduced number of international tourists but also to NGOs and aid workers who were increasingly coming into the country. This pivot involved offering long-term stays at discounted rates, providing workspace solutions, and hosting events and conferences related to the refugee crisis and humanitarian efforts.

Additionally, recognizing the importance of supporting the local community, the hotel began sourcing food and supplies from local producers impacted by the crisis, thereby contributing to the local economy and enhancing its sustainability ethos. They also implemented training programmes for refugees, offering employment opportunities within the hotel, thus integrating social responsibility into their business model. This adaptation not only helped the hotel to navigate through the economic downturn but also repositioned it as a socially responsible entity, attracting guests who value ethical and sustainable practices. Through innovation and community engagement, the hotel managed to sustain its operations and even build a new customer base, demonstrating resilience and adaptability in the face of adversity.

3.2 *Agriculture Sector*

Before the Syrian refugee crisis, Lebanon's agriculture sector played a crucial role in the country's economy and cultural identity, contributing significantly to GDP, employment, and food security (Hoteit et al., 2021). Renowned for its diverse agricultural produce, Lebanon boasted a rich tapestry of crops ranging from fruits and vegetables to tobacco and olives, thanks to its favourable climate and fertile lands. This sector not only supported local consumption but also served as a vital source of export income, with Lebanese products finding markets in Europe, the Arab world, and beyond (El Khansa, 2017). Small-scale farmers and agricultural cooperatives were the backbone of this sector, utilizing traditional farming methods passed down through generations, alongside modern techniques to enhance productivity. The industry faced challenges such as water scarcity, land degradation, and the need for technological advancement, but it remained resilient, supported by a network of local and international stakeholders committed to sustainable development (DeQuero-Navarro et al., 2020).

The onset of the Syrian refugee crisis introduced new dynamics to Lebanon's agriculture sector, impacting it in multifaceted ways. The sudden increase in the population led to a heightened demand for food, straining the existing agricultural supply chains and pushing up prices (Daher et al., 2021). While this increased demand presented an opportunity for local farmers to sell more produce, it also highlighted the challenges of scaling up production sustainably amidst limited resources. Moreover, the influx of refugees into rural areas, where many sought employment in agriculture, introduced labour market shifts. On one hand, the availability of cheaper labour provided some farmers the opportunity to reduce production costs (Turkmani & Hamade, 2020). However, this also led to tensions, as the increase in labour supply put downward pressure on wages, affecting the livelihoods of Lebanese farmworkers.

Additionally, the crisis exacerbated existing issues such as water scarcity and land competition, with increased agricultural activity putting further strain on Lebanon's natural resources. The need to balance immediate food security concerns with long-term sustainability goals became more pronounced, prompting discussions on agricultural policy, resource management, and the integration of refugees into the formal economy.

A case study that illustrates the local farming community's response to these challenges involves a cooperative in the Bekaa Valley, a region known for its agricultural productivity. Faced with the dual challenges of increased competition for resources and the need to scale up production, the cooperative adopted several innovative strategies. Recognizing the importance of sustainable resource management, they invested in water-saving irrigation technologies, which allowed them to increase production without exacerbating water scarcity. Additionally, they sought to improve the quality and marketability of their produce by adopting organic farming practices and obtaining certification, thus accessing higher-value markets locally and abroad.

To address labour market shifts, the cooperative implemented training programmes for both Lebanese farmers and Syrian refugees, focusing on sustainable farming techniques, resource management, and entrepreneurship. This approach not only helped in improving agricultural practices but also in fostering social cohesion by creating shared economic opportunities. By integrating refugees into their operations, the cooperative mitigated potential tensions and contributed to the community's resilience.

Moreover, the cooperative engaged in direct marketing strategies, bypassing traditional middlemen to sell their products directly to consumers, including through farmers' markets and online platforms. This not only ensured fairer prices for farmers but also raised awareness among consumers about the origins and quality of their food, strengthening the connection between producers and consumers.

Through these adaptations, the farming cooperative not only navigated the challenges posed by the refugee crisis but also positioned itself for long-term sustainability and growth. Their experience highlights the potential for resilience and innovation in the face of adversity, offering lessons on the importance of community-based approaches, sustainable resource management, and the integration of vulnerable populations into economic activities.

3.3 *Manufacturing Sector*

Prior to the Syrian refugee crisis, Lebanon's manufacturing sector was a dynamic component of the national economy, characterized by a diverse range of industries including food processing, textiles, chemicals, and metal products (Nahas, 2020). This sector not only provided a substantial number of jobs but also contributed significantly to Lebanon's GDP and export earnings (Baumann, 2021). Lebanese manufacturers prided themselves on the quality of their goods, leveraging the country's strategic location, skilled workforce, and entrepreneurial spirit to access markets in the Middle East, Africa, and beyond. However, the industry also faced challenges such as high operational costs, competition from abroad, and the need for modernization and technological upgrades to stay competitive in an increasingly globalized market (Ben Hassen, 2021).

The Syrian refugee crisis introduced new dynamics to Lebanon's manufacturing sector, presenting both operational challenges and market opportunities. On the operational side, manufacturers grappled with increased competition for resources, including water, energy, and labour. The influx of refugees led to a rise in labour supply, which, on one hand, reduced labour costs but, on the other hand, raised concerns about labour rights and working conditions (Borjas & Monras, 2017). Additionally, the increased demand for housing and services in areas with high refugee concentrations put pressure on infrastructure, affecting manufacturers' logistics and distribution networks (Kikano et al., 2021).

Despite these challenges, the crisis also presented opportunities for growth and innovation. The increased labour pool enabled some manufacturers to expand production lines or introduce new products at competitive prices (Lenner & Turner, 2019). Furthermore, the heightened demand within the local market, particularly for food, clothing, and construction materials, opened new avenues for businesses to cater to both the refugee population and the communities hosting them. Companies that adapted their operations and product offerings to meet these changing needs found new revenue streams and markets (Betts, 2021).

A case study highlighting adaptation within this sector involves a medium-sized enterprise specializing in the production of packaged foods. Before the crisis, the business primarily targeted the domestic market, with some exports to neighbouring countries. However, the refugee influx significantly increased demand for affordable, non-perishable food items. In response, the company adjusted its production strategy to include a range of products specifically designed to meet the needs and tastes of the refugee population, such as ready-to-eat meals and bulk packaging options.

Recognizing the importance of sustainability and community support, the business also initiated partnerships with local NGOs to distribute food packages to refugee camps, leveraging their distribution networks to reach new customers while contributing to relief efforts. This not only helped the company to expand its market presence but also enhanced its brand image and reputation within the community.

Moreover, the company invested in training programmes for both existing employees and newly hired refugees, focusing on improving productivity, food safety, and quality control. This approach not only improved operational efficiency but also facilitated the integration of refugees into the workforce, promoting social cohesion and stability.

Through these strategic adaptations, the manufacturing business was able to navigate the complexities of the new economic landscape, turning the challenges posed by the refugee crisis into opportunities for growth and social impact. This case study illustrates the potential for resilience and innovation in the manufacturing sector, emphasizing the importance of flexibility, community engagement, and sustainable practices in achieving business success amidst adversity.

4 Economic Adaptations and Innovations

4.1 Business Adaptation Strategies

The Syrian refugee crisis has prompted a significant re-evaluation of business practices across various sectors in Lebanon, leading to a wave of adaptations and innovations. Faced with unprecedented economic shifts, businesses have been compelled to rethink their strategies to remain viable and competitive. This period of adjustment has been characterized by a dual focus on overcoming immediate challenges and seizing new opportunities that have emerged from the crisis.

One of the most notable adaptations has been the diversification of products and services. Recognizing the changing needs of their consumer base, which now includes a significant number of refugees, businesses have tailored their offerings to cater to a broader demographic. This has involved not only adjusting product lines to meet different tastes and price sensitivities but also adopting more inclusive marketing strategies that appeal to a diverse clientele. For instance, food manufacturers have introduced products that cater to the dietary habits and preferences of the refugee population, while retail businesses have adjusted their inventory to include goods that are in higher demand by refugees and host communities alike (Nisbet et al., 2022).

Moreover, businesses have had to become more agile in their operations, often streamlining processes to reduce costs and improve efficiency. This agility has also meant adopting new technologies or innovative business models, such as online sales platforms, to access wider markets and reduce dependence on traditional, possibly disrupted supply chains. The digital transformation, accelerated by the crisis, has enabled businesses to maintain operations even in the face of logistical challenges and restrictions, connecting them with customers and suppliers in novel ways (Salameh, 2021).

Another significant adaptation has been the engagement in social responsibility initiatives, as businesses recognize the importance of supporting their communities in times of crisis. This has taken various forms, from partnering with NGOs to providing employment opportunities for refugees to participating in programmes aimed at improving local infrastructure and services (Kelley, 2017). Such initiatives not only contribute to the social fabric but also enhance the reputation of businesses, building loyalty among consumers who value corporate social responsibility.

The human resource aspect of business operations has also seen adjustments, with companies investing in training and development programmes to equip both their long-standing employees and newly hired refugees with the skills needed for the evolving market (Yüceer, 2018). This focus on workforce development not only helps businesses address current challenges but also prepares them for future growth, ensuring that they have a skilled and adaptable team.

In navigating the economic shifts prompted by the Syrian refugee crisis, businesses in Lebanon have demonstrated remarkable resilience and ingenuity. By diversifying their offerings, embracing technological innovation, engaging in community support, and focusing on workforce development, they have adapted to the new economic landscape. These strategies underscore the potential for businesses to not only survive but thrive in the face of adversity, contributing to economic recovery and resilience in crisis-affected regions.

4.2 *Innovative Economic Responses*

The influx of Syrian refugees into Lebanon has catalysed a wave of innovative economic responses, as stakeholders across sectors seek to capitalize on new opportunities and address the challenges posed by the crisis. One such response has been the emergence of social enterprises and start-ups focused on meeting the needs of both refugees and host communities (Alexandre et al., 2019). These ventures leverage business models that prioritize social impact alongside financial sustainability, addressing pressing issues such as access to education, healthcare, and employment. By providing innovative solutions to societal challenges, these enterprises not only contribute to economic growth but also foster social cohesion and resilience.

Furthermore, the crisis has spurred collaboration between public, private, and civil society actors to develop innovative approaches to humanitarian assistance and economic development. Initiatives such as public-private partnerships (PPPs) and impact investing have gained traction, bringing together stakeholders from diverse backgrounds to address complex challenges collaboratively. These partnerships leverage the resources and expertise of each sector to create sustainable solutions that benefit both refugees and host communities, fostering a more integrated and inclusive approach to economic development (Culbertson et al., 2016).

Additionally, the crisis has prompted a re-evaluation of traditional economic models, leading to the exploration of alternative approaches that prioritize resilience, sustainability, and inclusivity. Concepts such as circular economy principles, which emphasize resource efficiency, waste reduction, and closed-loop systems, have gained prominence as businesses seek to minimize their environmental impact while maximizing economic value (Muchangos, 2022). Similarly, the concept of inclusive economic growth, which aims to ensure that the benefits of economic development are equitably distributed across society, has become a central focus of policy discussions and initiatives.

Moreover, the crisis has accelerated the adoption of digital technologies and e-commerce platforms, creating new opportunities for businesses to reach customers and expand their markets. Online marketplaces, mobile payment systems, and digital marketing strategies have enabled businesses to overcome geographical barriers and connect with consumers both locally and globally (World Bank Group, 2016). This digital transformation has not only enhanced the resilience of businesses in the face of physical disruptions but has also democratized access to economic opportunities, particularly for marginalized communities such as refugees.

Innovative financing mechanisms have also emerged in response to the crisis, as stakeholders seek to mobilize capital for impactful investments in refugee-hosting communities. Social impact bonds, crowdfunding platforms, and microfinance initiatives are among the tools being utilized to channel funds towards projects that address critical needs such as infrastructure development, job creation, and skills training. By leveraging private sector investment for social good, these innovative financing mechanisms unlock new sources of capital while generating positive social and economic outcomes.

5 Implications for Policy and Recovery

In response to the immediate economic challenges posed by the Syrian refugee crisis, policymakers in Lebanon have implemented a range of short-term economic stabilization measures aimed at mitigating the impact on businesses, households, and public finances. One such measure has been the provision of financial assistance to vulnerable populations, including refugees and host communities, through social safety net programmes and humanitarian aid initiatives. These programmes provide cash transfers, food assistance, and other forms of support to those most affected by the crisis, helping to alleviate poverty, reduce food insecurity, and stimulate local demand. Additionally, policymakers have introduced measures to support businesses, such as tax incentives, grants, and loans, to help them weather the economic downturn and maintain operations. By providing financial relief and support to those most in need, these short-term stabilization measures aim to mitigate the immediate economic impacts of the crisis and lay the foundation for longer-term recovery and resilience.

Looking beyond immediate stabilization efforts, Lebanon is contemplating long-term economic growth strategies to harness the changes brought about by the Syrian refugee crisis for sustained development. One key aspect involves leveraging the skills and talents of the refugee population to bolster economic productivity and innovation. By investing in education and vocational training programmes tailored to the needs of both refugees and host communities, Lebanon can unlock the potential of its human capital, fostering entrepreneurship, job creation, and economic diversification. Furthermore, there is a growing recognition of the need to strengthen institutions, improve governance, and enhance the business environment to attract investment and promote sustainable growth. Policies aimed at reducing bureaucratic barriers, enhancing transparency, and combating corruption can help create a more conducive environment for business development and private sector investment. Additionally, there is an opportunity to capitalize on Lebanon's strategic location and connectivity to regional markets by investing in infrastructure development, trade facilitation, and economic integration initiatives. By adopting a comprehensive approach that addresses both short-term stabilization needs and long-term growth objectives, Lebanon can emerge stronger from the Syrian refugee crisis, building a more resilient and inclusive economy for the future.

6 Conclusion

This chapter offers a comprehensive examination of the economic impacts of the Syrian refugee crisis on Lebanon, shedding light on the multifaceted challenges and opportunities that have arisen as a result. Through a rigorous analysis of Lebanon's GDP and key economic sectors such as tourism, agriculture, and manufacturing, the chapter highlights the complex interplay of economic forces at play. From the initial strains on GDP growth rates to the nuanced shifts within specific industries, the economic ramifications of the crisis are both profound and far-reaching.

Moreover, the chapter underscores the resilience and adaptability of Lebanon's economy, as businesses and communities navigate the new economic landscape with innovation and ingenuity. Through case studies and examples, we see how local businesses have adapted their strategies to meet the changing needs of consumers and capitalize on emerging opportunities. These adaptive responses not only demonstrate the capacity for economic recovery but also offer insights into the broader implications for policy and long-term growth strategies.

Looking ahead, the chapter emphasizes the importance of a holistic approach to economic development, one that considers both short-term stabilization measures and long-term growth objectives. By leveraging the talents and potential of the refugee population, strengthening institutions, and investing in infrastructure and innovation, Lebanon can emerge from the crisis stronger and more resilient than before. Ultimately, this chapter contributes to a deeper understanding of the economic dynamics at play in Lebanon and provides valuable insights for policymakers, stakeholders, and scholars seeking to address the challenges of refugee crises and promote sustainable economic development.

References

Alexandre, L., Salloum, C., & Alalam, A. (2019). An investigation of migrant entrepreneurs: the case of Syrian refugees in Lebanon. *International Journal of Entrepreneurial Behavior & Research, 25*(5), 1147–1164.

Baumann, H. (2021). The causes, nature, and effect of the current crisis of Lebanese capitalism. In *Power-Sharing after Civil War* (pp. 61–77). Routledge.

Baylouny, A. M., & Klingseis, S. J. (2018). Water thieves or political catalysts? Syrian refugees in Jordan and Lebanon. *Middle East Policy, 25*(1), 104–123.

Beaujouan, J., & Rasheed, A. (Eds.). (2019). *Syrian crisis, Syrian refugees: Voices from Jordan and Lebanon*. Springer.

Ben Hassen, T. (2021). The state of the knowledge-based economy in the Arab world: Cases of Qatar and Lebanon. *EuroMed Journal of Business, 16*(2), 129–153.

Betts, A. (2021). *The wealth of refugees: How displaced people can build economies*. Oxford University Press.

Borjas, G. J., & Monras, J. (2017). The labour market consequences of refugee supply shocks. *Economic Policy, 32*(91), 361–413.

Culbertson, S., Oliker, O., Baruch, B., & Blum, I. (2016). *Rethinking coordination of services to refugees in urban areas: Managing the crisis in Jordan and Lebanon*. Rand Corporation.

Daher, B., Hamie, S., Pappas, K., Nahidul Karim, M., & Thomas, T. (2021). Toward resilient water-energy-food systems under shocks: Understanding the impact of migration, pandemics, and natural disasters. *Sustainability, 13*(16), 9402.

David, A., Marouani, M. A., Nahas, C., & Nilsson, B. (2020). The economics of the Syrian refugee crisis in neighbouring countries: The case of Lebanon. *Economics of Transition and Institutional Change, 28*(1), 89–109.

DeQuero-Navarro, B., Aoun Barakat, K., Shultz, C. J., Araque-Padilla, R. A., & Montero-Simo, M. J. (2020). From conflict to cooperation: A macromarketing view of sustainable and inclusive development in Lebanon and the Middle East. *Environmental Management, 66*, 232–247.

Dibeh, G., Fakih, A., & Marrouch, W. (2020). Tourism–growth nexus under duress: Lebanon during the Syrian crisis. *Tourism Economics, 26*(3), 353–370.

El Khansa, M. (2017). *Finding pathways for enhancing irrigated farming systems in Lebanon*. Doctoral dissertation, Université Montpellier.

Hameed, S. (2020). Political economy of rentierism in the Middle East and disruptions from the digital space. *Contemporary Review of the Middle East, 7*(1), 54–89.
Hoteit, M., Al-Atat, Y., Joumaa, H., Ghali, S. E., Mansour, R., Mhanna, R., Sayyed-Ahmad, F., Salameh, P., & Al-Jawaldeh, A. (2021). Exploring the impact of crises on food security in Lebanon: Results from a national cross-sectional study. *Sustainability, 13*(16), 8753.
Kelley, N. (2017). Responding to a refugee influx: Lessons from Lebanon. *Journal on Migration and Human Security, 5*(1), 82–104.
Kikano, F., Fauveaud, G., & Lizarralde, G. (2021). Policies of exclusion: The case of Syrian refugees in Lebanon. *Journal of Refugee Studies, 34*(1), 422–452.
Lenner, K., & Turner, L. (2019). Making refugees work? The politics of integrating Syrian refugees into the labor market in Jordan. *Middle East Critique, 28*(1), 65–95.
Mango, T. (2004). *Solidere: The battle for Beirut's Central District.* Doctoral dissertation, Massachusetts Institute of Technology.
Muchangos, L. S. D. (2022). Mapping the circular economy concept and the global south. *Circular Economy and Sustainability, 2*(1), 71–90.
Nahas, C. (2020). *An economy and a state for Lebanon.* Riad el-Rayyes Books.
Nisbet, C., Lestrat, K. E., & Vatanparast, H. (2022). Food security interventions among refugees around the globe: A scoping review. *Nutrients, 14*(3), 522.
Rabil, R. G. (2016). *The Syrian refugee crisis in Lebanon: The double tragedy of refugees and impacted host communities.* Lexington Books.
Rother, M. B., Pierre, M. G., Lombardo, D., Herrala, R., Toffano, M. P., Roos, M. E., Auclair, M. A., & Manasseh, M. K. (2016). *The economic impact of conflicts and the refugee crisis in the Middle East and North Africa.* International Monetary Fund.
Rowbotham, J. (2010). 'Sand and Foam': The changing identity of Lebanese tourism. *Journal of Tourism History, 2*(1), 39–53.
Salameh, E. (2021). *Digital transformation: Readiness of the Lebanese manufacturing industry.* Doctoral dissertation, Notre Dame University-Louaize.
Turkmani, N., & Hamade, K. (2020). *Dynamics of Syrian refugees in Lebanon's agriculture sector.* Issam Fares Institute for Public Policy and International Affairs at The American University of Beirut.
World Bank Group. (2016). *World development report 2016: Digital dividends.* World Bank Publications.
Yüceer, V. (2018). *The Role of NGOS in North Lebanon: Employment opportunities after the Syrian refugee crisis.* Master's thesis, Middle East Technical University.

CHAPTER 4

Labour Market Dynamics and Employment Challenges: Navigating the Impact of the Syrian Refugee Crisis in Lebanon

1 Introduction

The Syrian refugee crisis, a direct consequence of the civil war that began in Syria in 2011, has precipitated one of the most significant forced migrations in recent history. Lebanon, a neighbouring country with a population of approximately 6.8 million, has found itself at the epicentre of this migration crisis, hosting an estimated 1.5 million Syrian refugees. This influx, constituting nearly a quarter of Lebanon's pre-crisis population, has exerted unprecedented pressure on the country's socio-economic fabric, particularly its labour market.

The impact of the Syrian refugee crisis on Lebanon's labour market is multifaceted and profound, reshaping the employment landscape in ways that are both visible and subtle. Before the crisis, Lebanon's labour market was already characterized by high levels of unemployment and underemployment, particularly among its youth and female populations (Chaaban, 2013). The arrival of a large number of Syrian refugees, many of whom are willing to work at lower wages, has intensified competition for jobs, placing additional strain on an already fragile employment situation.

This intensified competition has had several immediate effects. First, it has led to a suppression of wages, as employers capitalize on the increased labour supply to offer lower wages. This wage suppression is particularly pronounced in sectors where Syrian refugees have found employment, such as agriculture, construction, and various forms of low-skilled work.

M. Zreik, *The Syrian Refugee Crisis and Lebanon's Economic Landscape*, https://doi.org/10.1007/978-3-031-68471-5_4

Second, the competition for jobs has exacerbated tensions between the host community and refugees, contributing to an environment of social and economic instability.

Moreover, the crisis has accelerated the expansion of the informal economy in Lebanon. The informal sector, which operates outside the purview of government regulation and taxation, has absorbed a significant portion of the refugee workforce. While this has provided immediate employment opportunities for many refugees, it has also posed long-term challenges for Lebanon's economic development and governance, including issues related to labour rights, job security, and public revenues.

This chapter explores the social and political ramifications of the refugee influx in Lebanon. It discusses how Lebanon's delicate sectarian balance has been affected and provides statistics on social services strain. Theoretical discussions on social integration and political stability are used to frame the empirical findings.

The chapter aims to provide an in-depth analysis of these dynamics, examining how the Syrian refugee crisis has transformed Lebanon's labour market and employment landscape. By dissecting the increased competition for jobs, the pressure on wages, and the expansion of the informal economy, the chapter seeks to offer insights into the immediate and long-term effects of the refugee influx on employment rates, wage levels, and overall labour market conditions. Through a combination of statistical data, policy analysis, and case studies, the narrative unfolds to reveal the complexities of employment in a context of massive forced migration, highlighting the challenges faced by both Lebanese citizens and Syrian refugees in navigating this new employment landscape.

2 Labour Market Before and After the Refugee Influx

2.1 Pre-crisis Labour Market Conditions

Before the onset of the Syrian refugee crisis, Lebanon's labour market was characterized by a set of unique challenges and dynamics that shaped its employment landscape. The country, with a diverse economy that includes banking, tourism, and services, has historically struggled with high levels of unemployment and underemployment, particularly among its youth and women (Jordan & Brun, 2021). The Lebanese labour market was marked by a significant mismatch between the skills offered by the workforce and those demanded by employers, leading to a scenario where a large segment of the population was either unemployed or engaged in jobs that did not fully utilize their skills and education.

The employment situation was further complicated by Lebanon's political instability and periodic security crises, which have historically deterred foreign investment and economic growth. This instability has often resulted in economic stagnation, with the country experiencing low levels of job creation, particularly in sectors that could offer high-quality employment opportunities (Chaaban, 2013). Consequently, a substantial portion of the Lebanese workforce sought employment opportunities abroad, in countries offering better economic prospects and stability (Nauffal & Skulte-Ouaiss, 2018).

Lebanon's labour market dynamics were also influenced by the presence of a substantial informal sector. Prior to the crisis, the informal economy comprised a wide range of activities, from street vending to unregistered businesses, employing a significant portion of the labour force. This sector, while offering employment opportunities, often did so at the cost of job security, labour rights, and access to social protection (Gatti et al., 2014). Workers in the informal economy were particularly vulnerable to economic shocks and lacked the safeguards that formal employment could provide.

Furthermore, the labour market in Lebanon was segmented along sectarian lines, with certain communities having preferential access to public sector jobs, a legacy of the country's complex confessional political system (Salamey, 2013). This segmentation contributed to inefficiencies and inequities in the labour market, exacerbating the challenges of unemployment and underemployment.

2.2 *Post-crisis Changes*

The influx of Syrian refugees into Lebanon, beginning in 2011, introduced a profound shift in the country's labour market dynamics, exacerbating existing challenges and introducing new ones. With an estimated 1.5 million Syrian refugees entering Lebanon, a country with a pre-crisis population of around 4.5 million, the labour market was suddenly inundated with a large number of individuals seeking employment, dramatically altering the employment landscape (Dbouk, 2020).

One of the most immediate and visible impacts of the refugee influx was the increased competition for jobs, particularly in sectors where barriers to entry were low. Syrian refugees, many of whom arrived with limited resources and in urgent need of income, often accepted work at lower wages, leading to downward pressure on wages across various sectors, including agriculture, construction, and low-skill service jobs (David et al., 2020). This wage suppression not only affected new entrants to the labour market but also existing workers, including Lebanese citizens and previous waves of migrants, who found themselves competing with refugees for the same jobs.

The expansion of the informal economy was another significant post-crisis change. The informal sector, already a substantial part of Lebanon's economy before the crisis, grew even larger as it absorbed a significant number of Syrian refugees (Rossis, 2011). This expansion was driven by several factors, including the refugees' need for immediate employment, the limited availability of formal jobs, and legal restrictions on their work rights. While informal employment provided a critical source of income for many refugees, it also raised concerns about labour rights, job security, and the long-term sustainability of this form of employment (Chen, 2023).

Moreover, the influx of refugees had a spatial impact on Lebanon's labour market, with certain areas of the country experiencing more acute effects than others. Regions hosting larger numbers of refugees saw more pronounced wage suppression and competition for jobs, leading to increased tensions between the host communities and refugees (Kikano et al., 2021). These tensions were not solely economic but were also fuelled by concerns over the strain on public services, infrastructure, and social cohesion.

The Syrian refugee crisis also prompted a re-evaluation of labour market policies and interventions in Lebanon. The government, in collaboration with international organizations, implemented various initiatives aimed at addressing the immediate impacts of the crisis and fostering longer-term labour market resilience (DeQuero-Navarro et al., 2020). These initiatives included efforts to regulate the informal economy, provide vocational training and employment services, and facilitate the integration of refugees into the labour market.

3 Competition for Jobs

3.1 Increased Job Competition

The entry of Syrian refugees into Lebanon's labour force has markedly heightened competition for jobs, a development with far-reaching implications for both the Lebanese economy and its social fabric. This increased competition is most acutely felt in sectors that traditionally employ low-skilled labour, such as agriculture, construction, and services, where the barriers to entry are relatively low. The refugees, many of whom were compelled to leave their homes and livelihoods behind, entered the Lebanese labour market willing to accept lower wages for work, primarily due to their urgent need for income and the absence of alternative employment opportunities. This willingness to work for lower pay has led to a significant shift in the labour market dynamics, affecting wages and employment opportunities for the entire workforce, including Lebanese nationals and previously established migrant communities.

The impact of this competition is multifaceted. First, it has led to wage suppression across several sectors. Employers, taking advantage of the increased supply of labour, have been able to offer lower wages, knowing that there is a ready pool of workers willing to accept these reduced rates (David et al., 2020). This situation has not only affected new job entrants but also existing employees, who have seen their bargaining power diminish in the face of an oversupplied labour market. In some instances, this has led to tensions between different groups of workers, as the struggle to secure and retain employment becomes increasingly fraught (Kikano et al., 2021).

Second, the heightened competition for jobs has exacerbated existing employment challenges within Lebanon. The country's labour market was already grappling with high unemployment rates, particularly among youth and women, even before the refugee crisis. The influx of Syrian refugees has made these challenges more severe, as more individuals vie for a limited number of job openings. This has had a ripple effect on the economy, contributing to increased unemployment and underemployment rates among the Lebanese population.

Moreover, the increased competition has also had social implications, fuelling tensions between Lebanese citizens and Syrian refugees. These tensions are not solely rooted in economic competition but are also intertwined with concerns over the strain on public services, infrastructure, and the perceived impact on Lebanese culture and society (Dibeh et al., 2019). The situation is further complicated by Lebanon's delicate sectarian balance, with the refugee influx sometimes perceived as threatening to alter the country's demographic and political equilibrium.

The government and various international organizations have recognized the need to address the heightened competition for jobs and its consequences. Policy responses have included efforts to regulate the employment of Syrian refugees, initiatives aimed at expanding employment opportunities for both Lebanese citizens and refugees, and programmes designed to enhance the skills and employability of the workforce. However, these measures face significant challenges, including limited resources, the scale of the refugee crisis, and the complexity of Lebanon's political and economic context.

3.2 *Impact on Lebanese Workers and Syrian Refugees*

The influx of Syrian refugees into Lebanon has had a profound impact on the labour market, with significant implications for both Lebanese workers and Syrian refugees. This situation presents a complex interplay of economic, social, and political dynamics that affect employment opportunities and living standards for both groups.

For Lebanese Workers

The entry of a large number of Syrian refugees into the labour market has intensified competition for jobs, particularly in sectors that traditionally employ low-skilled labour. This heightened competition has led to wage suppression in various industries, as employers take advantage of the increased supply of labour to offer lower wages. Lebanese workers, especially those in low-skilled positions, find themselves competing with refugees willing to accept lower pay for the same work, diminishing their bargaining power and potentially leading to reduced income and job insecurity (Habib et al., 2019). This situation exacerbates existing economic challenges faced by Lebanese workers, including high unemployment rates and the struggle to find stable, well-paying jobs.

Moreover, the perception of unfair competition has sometimes led to increased tensions between Lebanese communities and Syrian refugees. These tensions are not only economic but are also fuelled by concerns over the long-term social and demographic impact of the refugee presence in Lebanon. The strain on public services and infrastructure, already a challenge before the crisis, has been further exacerbated by the refugee influx, impacting the quality of life for Lebanese citizens.

For Syrian Refugees
For Syrian refugees, the primary motivation for entering the labour market is the urgent need for income to support themselves and their families. Many refugees have faced significant barriers to employment, including legal restrictions on their right to work, limited access to the formal labour market, and discrimination. As a result, a large number of refugees are employed in the informal sector, where they are vulnerable to exploitation, such as lower wages, poor working conditions, and a lack of job security and social protections (Habib et al., 2016). This precarious employment situation reflects the broader vulnerabilities faced by refugees, who often live in a state of legal and economic uncertainty.

While employment provides a critical lifeline for Syrian refugees, the nature of the jobs available to them—often low-skilled and poorly paid—limits their ability to achieve economic stability and integration. The lack of access to better employment opportunities constrains their prospects for long-term self-reliance and contributes to the perpetuation of poverty within the refugee community.

Comparative Analysis
The impact of the Syrian refugee crisis on employment opportunities presents a nuanced picture. For Lebanese workers, the crisis has led to increased competition for jobs and pressure on wages, exacerbating existing economic vulnerabilities. For Syrian refugees, while employment in Lebanon offers a crucial source of income, the predominantly low-skilled and informal nature of available work perpetuates their economic precarity.

Addressing the challenges faced by both Lebanese workers and Syrian refugees requires a multifaceted approach. Policies aimed at expanding economic opportunities, improving labour market regulation, and enhancing vocational training and education could help mitigate the adverse effects of competition and promote more inclusive economic growth. Furthermore, efforts to facilitate the legal integration of Syrian refugees into the labour market, coupled with measures to protect labour rights and improve working conditions, are essential for fostering a more stable and equitable employment landscape in Lebanon.

4 Wage Pressures and Employment Conditions

4.1 *Wage Suppression*

The Syrian refugee crisis has exerted significant downward pressure on wages in Lebanon, a phenomenon primarily driven by the substantial increase in labour supply. This wage suppression is a critical issue, impacting both the economic well-being of individuals and the broader socio-economic stability of the country. The influx of Syrian refugees, many of whom are willing to accept lower wages for employment, has created a labour market characterized by an oversupply of workers, especially in sectors that require low-skilled labour. This section delves into the dynamics of wage suppression, examining its causes, manifestations, and broader implications.

Causes of Wage Suppression

The primary cause of wage suppression in the context of the Syrian refugee crisis is the dramatic increase in the labour supply. With an estimated 1.5 million Syrian refugees entering Lebanon, a country with a pre-crisis population of just over 4 million, the labour market has been flooded with individuals seeking employment (Shellito, 2016). Many refugees, facing dire economic needs and limited legal rights to work, are compelled to accept whatever work they can find, often at wages below the market rate or the minimum wage. This willingness to work for lower pay has been seized upon by some employers, who see an opportunity to reduce labour costs, thereby exerting downward pressure on wages across various sectors (David et al., 2020).

Manifestations of Wage Suppression

Wage suppression has been most pronounced in sectors with high concentrations of refugee workers, such as agriculture, construction, and certain service industries. In these sectors, the abundance of labour willing to work for lower wages has led to a general decline in wage levels, affecting not only Syrian refugees but also Lebanese workers and migrants from other countries. The situation is exacerbated by the informal nature of much of the employment available to refugees, which operates outside the bounds of labour law and regulation, further depressing wages and working conditions (Maaroufi & Löw, 2019).

The impact of wage suppression extends beyond individual sectors, influencing the broader labour market and economy. Lower wages reduce the overall purchasing power of workers, potentially leading to decreased domestic consumption and economic stagnation (Lavoie & Stockhammer, 2013). Moreover, wage suppression can contribute to increased income inequality and social tensions, as workers struggle to meet their basic needs in the face of declining real incomes (Doussard, 2013).

Broader Implications

The downward pressure on wages due to the increased labour supply has several broader implications for Lebanon's socio-economic landscape. First, it contributes to heightened tensions between different segments of the population, as competition for jobs becomes more intense and the economic prospects of Lebanese workers are perceived to be undermined by the influx of refugees. Second, wage suppression challenges efforts to promote economic recovery and development in Lebanon, as lower wages can deter investment in sectors that rely on domestic consumption and limit the government's fiscal capacity through reduced tax revenues (Seguino, 2010).

Addressing the issue of wage suppression requires a comprehensive approach that balances the need to provide employment opportunities for refugees with the necessity of protecting the rights and livelihoods of all workers in Lebanon. Policies aimed at enhancing labour market regulation, enforcing minimum wage laws, and improving the working conditions in both the formal and informal sectors are crucial. Additionally, efforts to create new job opportunities through investment in infrastructure, education, and vocational training can help alleviate the pressure on wages by fostering economic growth and diversification.

4.2 Working Conditions

The labour market dynamics in Lebanon, significantly influenced by the Syrian refugee crisis, have not only impacted wages but also profoundly affected working conditions across both formal and informal sectors. The influx of refugees has exacerbated existing vulnerabilities within the labour market, leading to a deterioration of working conditions for many workers. This situation is particularly acute in the informal sector, which has expanded considerably as a result of the crisis, but it also affects formal employment to varying degrees. Understanding how these dynamics influence working conditions requires an examination of several key factors, including job security, labour rights, health and safety standards, and the overall quality of employment.

Deterioration of Working Conditions
The competitive pressure on jobs, coupled with the willingness of many refugees to accept employment under almost any conditions, has led to a notable deterioration in working conditions. In the informal sector, where a significant number of Syrian refugees find employment, conditions are often precarious, with little to no job security, absence of social protections, and exposure to exploitation. Workers in this sector frequently face long hours, low pay, and unsafe working environments, without access to legal recourse or protections typically afforded by formal employment (Ilcan et al., 2018).

Even within the formal sector, employers may exploit the increased labour supply to impose harsher conditions, knowing that workers have limited alternatives. This might include increased workloads, reduced benefits, and stricter controls on labour rights, such as collective bargaining and the right to organize. The fear of job loss compels many workers to accept these conditions, undermining labour standards and contributing to a race to the bottom in terms of employment quality.

Impact on Health and Safety
One of the most concerning aspects of the deterioration in working conditions is the compromise on health and safety standards. In sectors like construction and agriculture, which have seen a significant influx of refugee labour, reports of unsafe working conditions, accidents, and lack of protective measures have increased (Moyce & Schenker, 2018). The informal nature of much of the work undertaken by refugees means that such incidents are often underreported and unaddressed, posing significant risks to worker health and safety.

Social and Economic Implications
The decline in working conditions has broader social and economic implications. For workers, the combination of low wages and poor working conditions can lead to a cycle of poverty and exploitation, affecting their health, well-being, and ability to support their families. This situation also has implications for social cohesion, as resentment and tension may grow between different groups competing for the same low-quality jobs.

Moreover, the degradation of labour standards can have long-term economic consequences. It can deter skilled workers and professionals, undermine productivity, and discourage investment in sectors with poor labour practices. This undermines efforts towards sustainable economic development and the creation of decent work for all.

Towards Improved Working Conditions
Addressing the challenges of working conditions in Lebanon, especially in the context of the refugee crisis, requires concerted efforts from the government, international organizations, employers, and labour unions. Key measures include strengthening labour law enforcement, promoting decent work standards, ensuring access to legal recourse for workers in the informal sector, and improving occupational health and safety standards. Additionally, policies aimed at economic diversification and the creation of quality jobs can help reduce the reliance on informal employment and improve working conditions across the board.

5 Expansion of the Informal Economy

5.1 Growth of Informal Employment

The expansion of the informal economy in Lebanon, particularly in the wake of the Syrian refugee crisis, is a phenomenon with deep-rooted causes and wide-ranging implications. The informal sector, characterized by unregulated work environments, lack of formal contracts, and absence of social protections, has burgeoned under the pressures of increased labour supply and economic strain. This growth is driven by several factors, each contributing to the complexity of the labour market and the challenges faced by both workers and policymakers.

Drivers of Informal Employment Growth
One of the primary reasons for the expansion of informal employment is the influx of Syrian refugees into Lebanon's labour market. Many refugees, facing legal restrictions on their ability to work formally and in urgent need of income, have turned to the informal sector (Habib et al., 2019). The informal economy offers easier entry for those without the legal right to work or who are unable to secure formal employment due to lack of recognition of qualifications or discrimination.

Additionally, the pre-existing condition of Lebanon's labour market, characterized by high unemployment and underemployment rates, especially among youth and women, has made the informal sector a critical buffer for many Lebanese citizens as well. The informal sector often provides the only available employment opportunities for a significant portion of the population, further fuelling its growth.

Economic challenges and political instability in Lebanon have also played a significant role in driving the expansion of informal employment. Businesses operating within the formal sector face numerous hurdles, including high taxes, complex regulations, and political uncertainty, which discourage formal employment creation and encourage a shift towards informality as a means of cost reduction and risk mitigation (Alloush et al., 2013).

Implications of Informal Economy Expansion

The growth of the informal economy has significant implications for workers, the economy, and society at large. Workers in the informal sector are typically subject to lower wages, poor working conditions, and a lack of job security and social protections, such as health insurance and retirement benefits. This precariousness exacerbates vulnerabilities, particularly for refugees and marginalized Lebanese populations, trapping many in cycles of poverty and exploitation.

From an economic perspective, the expansion of the informal sector undermines the state's fiscal capacity, as informal businesses and workers do not contribute to tax revenues. This limits the government's ability to invest in public services and infrastructure, further straining the social contract and contributing to public discontent.

Moreover, the prevalence of informal employment challenges efforts to regulate the labour market and enforce labour standards, complicating policy responses to labour market dynamics and economic crises. The informal economy's expansion reflects deeper structural issues within Lebanon's economy and labour market, necessitating comprehensive strategies that address both the symptoms and root causes of informality.

5.2 *Challenges and Opportunities*

The expansion of the informal economy in Lebanon, while providing immediate employment opportunities for Syrian refugees and Lebanese citizens alike, presents a complex set of challenges and opportunities for economic integration and regulation. Navigating this landscape requires a nuanced understanding of the informal sector's impact on workers, the economy, and broader societal dynamics.

Challenges of the Informal Economy

One of the primary challenges posed by the informal economy is the vulnerability of workers. Individuals employed in informal settings often lack access to social protections, such as health insurance, pensions, and safe working conditions, exposing them to greater risks of exploitation and poverty (Kabeer, 2014). This vulnerability is exacerbated for Syrian refugees, who may also face legal barriers to formal employment, further limiting their options.

The informal economy also complicates efforts to regulate the labour market and enforce labour standards. The absence of formal contracts and oversight mechanisms makes it difficult to protect workers' rights and ensure fair labour practices. This challenge is intertwined with the broader issue of state capacity and governance, as effective regulation requires both the legal framework and the institutional capacity to enforce it.

Economically, the informal sector poses challenges for fiscal policy and economic development. Informal businesses and workers do not contribute to tax revenues, limiting the government's ability to fund public services and infrastructure (Brinkerhoff & Brinkerhoff, 2011). Moreover, the predominance of informal employment can hinder economic growth by discouraging investment in more productive and innovative sectors of the economy.

Opportunities for Economic Integration and Regulation

Despite these challenges, the informal economy also presents opportunities for economic integration and regulation. Recognizing the role of the informal sector in providing livelihoods for many, strategies can be developed to formalize these activities, bringing them into the regulatory and fiscal frameworks.

One approach is to simplify the process of formalization, reducing the costs and bureaucratic hurdles associated with registering businesses and employment. This could include tax incentives for small businesses to formalize, streamlined registration processes, and support services for entrepreneurs.

Efforts to improve the legal framework for refugees' right to work can also facilitate their integration into the formal economy. This requires balancing the need to protect the labour market for Lebanese citizens with the economic benefits of integrating refugees into the workforce, such as filling labour shortages and fostering economic dynamism.

Furthermore, targeted vocational training and education programmes can enhance the skills of both Lebanese citizens and Syrian refugees, improving their employability in the formal sector and contributing to economic growth. Such programmes can be designed to meet the needs of emerging sectors with potential for job creation and innovation.

6 Policy Responses and Interventions

In addressing the labour market challenges precipitated by the Syrian refugee crisis, the Lebanese government, alongside international organizations, has embarked on a series of policy measures and interventions. These initiatives are designed to mitigate the adverse effects of the crisis on employment and wages, and to foster a more resilient and inclusive labour market. The response strategies encompass a range of approaches, from regulatory adjustments to support programmes aimed at enhancing the skills and employability of both Lebanese citizens and Syrian refugees.

A key aspect of these efforts has involved adapting the legal framework to better regulate the employment of Syrian refugees, aiming to balance the need for labour market protection for Lebanese citizens with the economic realities brought about by the refugee influx (Atallah & Mahdi, 2017). This has included measures such as limiting refugee employment to certain sectors and implementing work permit regulations. Additionally, the government and its international partners have invested in vocational training and skill development programmes (Dagher & Nehme, 2021). These initiatives seek to align the skills of the workforce with the demands of the labour market, particularly in sectors identified as having growth potential or facing labour shortages. The intention behind these programmes is not only to improve immediate employment prospects but also to lay the groundwork for longer-term economic development and integration.

Furthermore, efforts have been made to stimulate job creation through support for small and medium-sized enterprises (SMEs), which are viewed as a vital engine of economic growth and employment. Financial assistance, training, and access to markets are among the forms of support provided to help these businesses thrive and expand their workforce (Hamdar et al., 2017). International organizations have also played a crucial role in funding and implementing projects aimed at infrastructure development and community support, which indirectly contribute to job creation and economic stability (Al Shaher & Zreik, 2022).

While these policy responses and interventions have had some success in addressing the immediate needs of the labour market and supporting vulnerable populations, their effectiveness has been mixed, and several limitations have become apparent. One of the critical challenges has been the scale of the crisis and the sheer number of individuals needing assistance, which has often outstripped the resources and capacity available for these programmes. Moreover, the regulatory measures, such as work permit restrictions, have had unintended consequences. They have sometimes pushed more refugees into the informal economy, where they are less protected and more vulnerable to exploitation, thus exacerbating some of the issues these policies aimed to mitigate.

The vocational training and skills development programmes, while beneficial, have sometimes struggled to achieve alignment with labour market needs, resulting in mismatches between the skills taught and those in demand. This misalignment can limit the effectiveness of such programmes in enhancing employability and integrating participants into the labour market. Additionally, the focus on short-term economic relief has at times overshadowed the need for longer-term strategic planning for economic development and labour market resilience, which is essential for addressing the underlying structural issues within the Lebanese economy.

The support for SMEs, critical for job creation, has also faced challenges. These include the difficult economic environment in Lebanon, characterized by political instability, infrastructural deficits, and financial constraints, which can hinder business growth and the sustainability of employment gains. Furthermore, while international organizations have provided significant support, coordination challenges and the complexity of implementing projects in a volatile environment can limit their impact.

7 Case Studies: Local Responses and Adaptations

In the face of the labour market challenges induced by the Syrian refugee crisis, several local communities and businesses in Lebanon have devised innovative responses and adaptations, showcasing resilience and creativity. One notable case involves a community-led initiative in the Bekaa Valley, where local Lebanese and Syrian refugees collaborated to establish a cooperative farm. This project not only provided employment opportunities for both communities but also fostered social cohesion by working towards a common goal. The cooperative's success lies in its ability to utilize the agricultural skills of Syrian refugees, alongside the local knowledge of Lebanese farmers, to enhance productivity and sustainability.

Another example comes from a tech start-up in Beirut, which launched a platform to connect skilled refugees with remote working opportunities in the digital sector. Recognizing the untapped potential of the refugee population, this initiative provides training in digital skills, language proficiency, and professional development. It has successfully placed numerous participants in jobs that offer not just a stable income but also a sense of dignity and purpose. These case studies exemplify how local responses, grounded in the specific needs and capacities of communities, can effectively address labour market challenges, providing a blueprint for broader, more inclusive strategies.

8 Conclusion

The exploration of labour market dynamics and employment challenges in Lebanon, in the context of the Syrian refugee crisis, reveals a complex landscape shaped by increased competition for jobs, wage pressures, and the expansion of the informal economy. The influx of Syrian refugees has undeniably transformed the Lebanese labour market, introducing both significant challenges and opportunities for policy responses and interventions.

Government and international efforts, alongside innovative local initiatives, have sought to mitigate the adverse effects of this transformation. These efforts have ranged from regulatory adjustments and vocational training programmes to support for small and medium-sized enterprises and community-led projects. While these interventions have achieved some success in addressing the immediate impacts of the crisis, they have also encountered limitations, including resource constraints, regulatory challenges, and the need for better alignment with labour market demands.

The case studies presented highlight the potential of local responses and business adaptations in addressing labour market challenges, demonstrating the importance of community engagement and innovative approaches in fostering economic resilience and integration. These examples serve as a testament to the capacity of local actors to devise effective solutions that cater to the specific needs and opportunities within their communities.

References

Al Shaher, S., & Zreik, M. (2022). The impact of job characteristics and value congruence on employee retention: An empirical study from Lebanon. *The Journal of Asian Finance, Economics and Business (JAFEB), 9*(3), 171–180.

Alloush, M., Chartouni, C., Gatti, R., & Silva, J. (2013). Informality and exclusion: Evidence from matched employer-employee data for Lebanon and Syria. *IZA Journal of Labor Policy, 2*, 1–18.

Atallah, S., & Mahdi, D. (2017). *Law and politics of "safe zones" and forced return to Syria: Refugee politics in Lebanon*. The Lebanese Center for Policy Studies.

Brinkerhoff, D. W., & Brinkerhoff, J. M. (2011). Public–private partnerships: Perspectives on purposes, publicness, and good governance. *Public Administration and Development, 31*(1), 2–14.

Chaaban, J. (2013). *Expanding youth opportunities in the Arab region*. United Nations Development Programme, Regional Bureau for Arab States.

Chen, M. A. (2023). Informal livelihood strategies of Syrian refugees in Jordan and Lebanon: A conceptual framework and comparative perspective. In *Refugee resilience and adaptation in the Middle East* (pp. 36–61). Routledge.

Dagher, L., & Nehme, R. (2021). Can Lebanon's economy be saved? A plan for revival. *Middle East Policy, 28*(1), 123–134.

David, A., Marouani, M. A., Nahas, C., & Nilsson, B. (2020). The economics of the Syrian refugee crisis in neighbouring countries: The case of Lebanon. *Economics of Transition and Institutional Change, 28*(1), 89–109.

Dbouk, M. (2020). *Evolution and prospects of the economy of Lebanon*. Doctoral dissertation, Politecnico di Torino.

DeQuero-Navarro, B., Aoun Barakat, K., Shultz, C. J., Araque-Padilla, R. A., & Montero-Simo, M. J. (2020). From conflict to cooperation: A macromarketing view of sustainable and inclusive development in Lebanon and the Middle East. *Environmental Management, 66*, 232–247.

Dibeh, G., Fakih, A., & Marrouch, W. (2019). Employment and skill mismatch among youth in Lebanon. *International Journal of Manpower, 40*(8), 1438–1457.

Doussard, M. (2013). *Degraded work: The struggle at the bottom of the labor market*. University of Minnesota Press.

Gatti, R., Angel-Urdinola, D. F., Silva, J., & Bodor, A. (2014). *Striving for better jobs: The challenge of informality in the Middle East and North Africa*. World Bank Publications.

Habib, R. R., Mikati, D., Hojeij, S., El Asmar, K., Chaaya, M., & Zurayk, R. (2016). Associations between poor living conditions and multi-morbidity among Syrian migrant agricultural workers in Lebanon. *The European Journal of Public Health, 26*(6), 1039–1044.

Habib, R. R., Ziadee, M., Abi Younes, E., Harastani, H., Hamdar, L., Jawad, M., & El Asmar, K. (2019). Displacement, deprivation and hard work among Syrian refugee children in Lebanon. *BMJ Global Health, 4*(1), e001122.

Hamdar, B. C., Najjar, R., & Karameh, K. (2017). The Lebanese perception of the impact of small & medium enterprises (SMEs) on the national economy. *Journal of Economics and Public Finance, 3*(3), 330–342.

Ilcan, S., Rygiel, K., & Baban, F. (2018). The ambiguous architecture of precarity: Temporary protection, everyday living and migrant journeys of Syrian refugees. *International Journal of Migration and Border Studies, 4*(1–2), 51–70.

Jordan, Z., & Brun, C. (2021). Vital conjunctures in compound crises: Conceptualising young People's education trajectories in protracted displacement in Jordan and Lebanon. *Social Sciences, 10*(7), 241.

Kabeer, N. (2014). *Gender & social protection strategies in the informal economy.* Routledge India.

Kikano, F., Fauveaud, G., & Lizarralde, G. (2021). Policies of exclusion: The case of Syrian refugees in Lebanon. *Journal of Refugee Studies, 34*(1), 422–452.

Lavoie, M., & Stockhammer, E. (2013). Wage-led growth: Concept, theories and policies. In *Wage-led growth: An equitable strategy for economic recovery* (pp. 13–39). Palgrave Macmillan.

Maaroufi, M., & Löw, N. (2019). Challenging infrastructures of domestic labor: Implications for labor organizing in Lebanon and Belgium. *Journal of Labor and Society, 22*(4), 853–873.

Moyce, S. C., & Schenker, M. (2018). Migrant workers and their occupational health and safety. *Annual Review of Public Health, 39*, 351–365.

Nauffal, D., & Skulte-Ouaiss, J. (2018). Quality higher education drives employability in the Middle East. *Education + Training, 60*(9), 1057–1069.

Rossis, N. (2011). *The informal economy in Lebanon: Dangers and benefits.* Doctoral dissertation, Durham University.

Salamey, I. (2013). *The government and politics of Lebanon.* Routledge.

Seguino, S. (2010). The global economic crisis, its gender and ethnic implications, and policy responses. *Gender and Development, 18*(2), 179–199.

Shellito, K. (2016). *The economic effect of refugee crises on host countries and implications for the Lebanese case.* Doctoral dissertation, University of Pennsylvania.

CHAPTER 5

Inflationary Spirals and Cost of Living Challenges: The Economic Consequences of the Syrian Refugee Crisis in Lebanon

1 Introduction

The chapter begins by setting the stage for a comprehensive examination of the inflationary pressures and cost of living challenges that Lebanon has encountered in the wake of the Syrian refugee crisis. It highlights the pivotal role that the sudden influx of refugees has played in exacerbating existing economic vulnerabilities, leading to significant socio-economic repercussions for both the host communities and the refugees themselves. The introduction underscores the urgency and importance of understanding these inflationary dynamics, as they have not only strained the resources and infrastructure of Lebanon but also compounded the hardships faced by the Syrian refugees seeking sanctuary.

Lebanon, a country already grappling with its own set of economic and political challenges, found itself at the forefront of one of the most significant refugee crises of the twenty-first century. The arrival of millions of Syrian refugees, fleeing the devastating conflict in their homeland, introduced unprecedented demands on the Lebanese economy, particularly in the housing market, food sector, and other essential services. This chapter aims to dissect the multifaceted nature of these economic pressures, drawing attention to how the increased demand for goods and services has led to widespread price hikes and intensified the cost of living.

Through a meticulous analysis, the chapter will explore how these inflationary trends have permeated various sectors of the Lebanese economy,

M. Zreik, *The Syrian Refugee Crisis and Lebanon's Economic Landscape*, https://doi.org/10.1007/978-3-031-68471-5_5

affecting everything from the price of a loaf of bread to the cost of renting a home. It will delve into the direct impact these price increases have had on the everyday lives of people, highlighting the growing struggle to afford basic necessities and maintain a decent standard of living. The introduction sets the stage for a deeper exploration of the broader economic implications of these trends, including shifts in consumption patterns, a rise in poverty rates, and the overall stability of Lebanon's economy.

The focus of this chapter is the range of responses from the international community and regional players to Lebanon's refugee situation. It outlines the aid received, policy measures taken, and the effectiveness of these actions, using international relations and humanitarian aid theories to analyse the adequacy of the response.

The narrative laid out in this introduction emphasizes the complexity of the situation, pointing to the Syrian refugee crisis not just as a humanitarian issue but also as a catalyst for economic strain that poses significant challenges to Lebanon's economic stability. The chapter promises to offer a balanced view, incorporating quantitative data, policy analysis, and real-life case studies to paint a comprehensive picture of the inflationary landscape. It aims to provide valuable insights into potential policy responses and mitigation strategies that could alleviate the economic burdens faced by both Lebanese citizens and Syrian refugees, setting a tone of inquiry and solution-seeking that will permeate the subsequent sections.

2 Inflationary Trends Post-refugee Influx

2.1 Overview of Inflationary Pressures

In the aftermath of the Syrian refugee influx into Lebanon, the country has faced significant inflationary pressures, impacting various sectors of the economy and altering the cost structure of essential goods and services. This period, marked by a dramatic increase in demand against a backdrop of limited supply, has led to widespread price hikes, deeply affecting the economic landscape. The surge in population, as Syrian refugees sought safety and shelter, introduced a substantial increase in consumption needs, ranging from housing to food, healthcare, and education, thereby exerting upward pressure on prices.

Statistical data reveals a stark transformation in the inflationary trends, with key sectors experiencing varying degrees of price increases. The housing market, one of the most directly impacted sectors, saw rental prices soar as demand outstripped supply, making affordable housing increasingly scarce for both refugees and local residents alike (Kikano et al., 2021). Similarly, the food sector faced heightened demand, leading to price surges that have made basic foodstuffs and essential goods less accessible to a significant portion of the population (Sumpf et al., 2016). This inflationary environment extends beyond housing and food, affecting services and goods across the board, thereby straining household budgets and exacerbating living costs.

The implications of these inflationary pressures are multifaceted, affecting not only the economic stability of Lebanon but also the social fabric of its communities. The rising cost of living has placed a considerable burden on Lebanese citizens, many of whom were already navigating a challenging economic landscape prior to the refugee crisis. For Syrian refugees, the situation is particularly dire, as they confront the dual challenges of displacement and the escalating cost of basic necessities, further complicating their struggle for survival and integration into Lebanese society.

This period of inflationary trends underscores the complex interplay between supply and demand dynamics, economic policies, and external shocks, such as the refugee influx. It highlights the need for a nuanced understanding of inflation's root causes and its broader implications for society. Moreover, the data points to the urgency of implementing effective policy measures and interventions to mitigate the impact of inflation, ensure economic stability, and support the most vulnerable populations. The analysis of these trends serves as a crucial foundation for exploring the economic implications of the refugee crisis in Lebanon, providing a context for discussing policy responses and mitigation strategies in subsequent sections of the chapter.

2.2 *Sector-Specific Inflation*

The inflationary impact of the Syrian refugee crisis in Lebanon has not been uniform across all sectors; instead, it has manifested differently within various areas of the economy, notably in housing, food, and services. Each sector has faced its unique set of challenges and pressures, leading to distinct inflationary patterns that collectively contribute to the broader economic strain experienced by the country.

In the housing sector, the sudden and substantial increase in demand for shelter, driven by the influx of refugees, has led to a sharp rise in rental prices (Baumann, 2021). This escalation has not only made it increasingly difficult for refugees to find affordable housing but has also impacted Lebanese citizens, many of whom have found themselves priced out of their own housing markets. The competition for limited housing resources has exacerbated existing shortages, pushing prices upward and contributing to a significant sector-specific inflationary trend.

The food sector has similarly been affected, with the increased population leading to heightened demand for food and essential goods. This surge in demand has come up against the constraints of supply chains, which, due to various factors including logistical challenges and import dependencies, have struggled to keep pace. As a result, food prices have seen considerable increases, impacting the affordability and accessibility of basic nutrition for both the local and refugee populations (Jomaa et al., 2021). This inflationary pressure within the food sector not only affects immediate consumption but also has broader implications for nutritional health and food security.

Services, encompassing a wide range of economic activities from healthcare to education and transportation, have also witnessed inflationary pressures. The increased demand for these services, coupled with the strain on infrastructure and resources, has led to higher costs and, in some cases, a reduction in the quality of services provided (Dahham et al., 2023). This has placed additional burdens on all residents in Lebanon, affecting their access to essential services and overall quality of life.

The sector-specific inflation experienced in Lebanon in the wake of the refugee crisis highlights the complex interdependencies within the economy. It underscores the challenges of managing supply and demand dynamics in a crisis situation, where the needs of a significantly increased population must be met under constrained resources. The detailed examination of inflation within these key sectors not only sheds light on the direct economic impacts of the refugee crisis but also serves as a basis for understanding the broader economic and social challenges facing Lebanon. It emphasizes the need for targeted interventions and policies that can address the unique inflationary pressures within each sector, aiming to mitigate their impact and ensure the stability and well-being of both the Lebanese and refugee populations.

3 Impact on Cost of Living

3.1 Housing Market Pressures

The surge in housing prices in Lebanon, exacerbated by the influx of Syrian refugees, has had a profound impact on the cost of living for both the refugee population and local residents, fundamentally altering the landscape of affordability and accessibility in the housing market. This significant increase in demand for housing, precipitated by the arrival of a large number of refugees, has placed immense pressure on the already limited housing stock, leading to skyrocketing rental prices and making it increasingly difficult for individuals and families to secure affordable accommodation.

For Syrian refugees, many of whom arrived with limited resources and continue to face barriers to employment and income generation, the rising cost of housing has compounded their vulnerability, pushing decent housing out of reach for many. The struggle to find affordable shelter often forces refugees into overcrowded, substandard living conditions, exacerbating their already precarious situation and further marginalizing them from the host community (Habib et al., 2020).

Local Lebanese residents have not been immune to these pressures. The competition for housing has driven up prices to levels that many locals find unaffordable, leading to displacement and increased financial strain for families that have lived in these communities for generations. This has contributed to tensions between the host community and refugees, as both groups vie for the same scarce resources, underlining the broader social and economic challenges posed by the refugee crisis (Marrouch & Sayour, 2021).

The impact of housing market pressures on the cost of living extends beyond the immediate challenge of securing shelter. It influences a wide range of economic and social outcomes, from education and health to employment opportunities. Families spending a disproportionate amount of their income on housing may have to forego other essentials, such as nutritious food, healthcare, and education, further entrenching cycles of poverty and disadvantage.

Moreover, the housing affordability crisis has implications for urban development and infrastructure in Lebanon. The rapid increase in demand for housing has led to unplanned and often unsafe expansions of urban areas, straining public services and infrastructure. This, in turn, affects the overall quality of life and can lead to long-term environmental and social issues, such as increased pollution and social segregation.

The surge in housing prices in the context of the Syrian refugee crisis in Lebanon highlights the intricate connection between housing affordability and broader economic and social stability. It underscores the need for comprehensive policy responses that address the root causes of housing market pressures, including initiatives to increase the supply of affordable housing, support income generation for vulnerable groups, and ensure equitable access to resources. Addressing these challenges is critical not only for mitigating the immediate impact on the cost of living but also for fostering long-term resilience and cohesiveness within Lebanese society and among its refugee population.

3.2 *Food and Essential Goods*

The escalation in prices for food and other essential goods in Lebanon, in the wake of the Syrian refugee crisis, has had a significant impact on household budgets and living standards, affecting both the local and refugee populations. This price inflation in basic necessities is a direct consequence of increased demand coupled with supply constraints, leading to a situation where the cost of everyday items has risen sharply (Khalil & Dagher, 2024). Such inflation deeply influences the economic well-being of families, forcing them to adjust their spending habits and, in many cases, compromise on the quality and quantity of food and goods they can afford.

For many households, food constitutes a substantial portion of monthly expenditure. As prices have increased, families have found themselves caught in a challenging position, having to allocate a larger share of their income to purchase the same, or even reduced, amounts of food (Kharroubi et al., 2021). This shift has direct implications for nutritional health, with more and more families unable to afford a balanced diet. The situation is particularly dire for the most vulnerable segments of the population, including low-income Lebanese families and Syrian refugees, who may already be struggling with limited financial resources. The rising cost of food exacerbates food insecurity, a condition that can lead to malnutrition and associated health problems.

Beyond food, the price inflation of other essential goods, such as hygiene products, clothing, and fuel, further strains household budgets (Corriero et al., 2022). As these items become more expensive, families are forced to make difficult choices, often prioritizing immediate necessities over other important needs. This can lead to a decrease in overall living standards, with long-term consequences for health, education, and well-being. The impact is pervasive, affecting nearly all aspects of daily life and contributing to increased stress and anxiety among affected populations.

The implications of these price increases extend beyond individual households, affecting broader socio-economic dynamics within Lebanon. As families divert more of their income to cover basic needs, there is less available for savings, investment, or spending on services, which can dampen economic growth and exacerbate poverty levels. Moreover, the strain on household budgets can fuel social tensions, particularly in a context where resources are scarce and competition is fierce between different groups for access to affordable goods and services.

The rising cost of food and essential goods in Lebanon illustrates the complex challenges faced by the country in the wake of the Syrian refugee crisis. It highlights the interconnectedness of economic factors, such as inflation and supply chain dynamics, with social outcomes, including health, education, and social cohesion. Addressing these challenges requires a multi-faceted approach that encompasses not only economic measures to stabilize prices and improve supply chains but also social policies to support vulnerable families and ensure that basic needs are met. Such efforts are crucial for mitigating the immediate impact on household budgets and living standards, as well as for laying the groundwork for long-term social and economic stability in Lebanon.

4 Economic Implications

The inflationary pressures stemming from the Syrian refugee crisis have had profound implications for the Lebanese economy, notably through their impact on consumption patterns and an exacerbation of poverty and economic vulnerability among both Lebanese citizens and Syrian refugees. These economic shifts offer a glimpse into the broader socio-economic challenges Lebanon faces, underlining the urgency for targeted interventions.

The alteration in consumption patterns within the Lebanese economy is a direct consequence of the inflationary pressures that have escalated the cost of living. As prices for basic necessities such as food, housing, and services have surged, households have been compelled to adjust their spending habits significantly. Families across the socio-economic spectrum find themselves allocating a larger portion of their income to cover essential needs, with discretionary spending taking a backseat. This shift in consumer behaviour reflects a broader trend of decreased consumer confidence and spending power, which, in turn, affects the overall economic activity. Businesses, especially those reliant on discretionary spending, face reduced demand for their products and services, leading to a potential slowdown in economic growth and employment opportunities (Elia et al., 2023). The impact on consumption patterns is thus both a reflection of and a contributor to the broader economic challenges facing Lebanon, highlighting a cycle of decreased spending and economic contraction that is difficult to break without comprehensive policy interventions.

Concurrently, the rise in poverty rates and increased economic vulnerability represent some of the most pressing economic implications of the crisis. The inflationary environment, compounded by limited access to employment opportunities for refugees and a stagnating economy for locals, has pushed a significant portion of the population into poverty or near-poverty conditions (Jones, 2023). The Lebanese citizens, many of whom were already facing economic hardships prior to the refugee influx, have seen their economic stability further eroded, with an increasing number struggling to meet basic needs. For Syrian refugees, the lack of legal employment opportunities, combined with the high cost of living, has resulted in severe economic distress, with many families relying on humanitarian aid to survive (BouChabke & Haddad, 2021). This heightened economic vulnerability not only undermines the immediate well-being of affected populations but also has long-term implications for social cohesion, public health, and economic recovery. The increasing poverty rates reflect a deepening divide between different segments of the population, exacerbating tensions and highlighting the need for targeted social and economic policies to address the root causes of poverty and economic instability.

The dual impact of altered consumption patterns and increased poverty rates underscores the complex economic challenges Lebanon faces in the wake of the Syrian refugee crisis. These challenges highlight the interconnected nature of inflation, consumer behaviour, economic growth, and social stability. Addressing these issues requires a multi-pronged approach that combines macroeconomic stabilization efforts with targeted support for vulnerable populations. Strategies to enhance economic resilience, support small and medium-sized enterprises, create employment opportunities, and provide social protection for the most at-risk groups are critical components of a comprehensive response to mitigate the economic implications of the crisis and foster a more inclusive and sustainable economic recovery.

5 Policy Responses and Mitigation Strategies

5.1 *Government and International Actions*

In response to the multifaceted economic challenges posed by the Syrian refugee crisis and the resultant inflationary pressures, a combination of government and international actions has been initiated with the aim of curbing inflation and supporting the affected populations in Lebanon. These policy measures and interventions are designed to address both the immediate economic impacts and the underlying vulnerabilities that have been exacerbated by the crisis.

The Lebanese government, in collaboration with international organizations and donor countries, has embarked on a series of policy initiatives aimed at stabilizing the economy and providing relief to those most affected by the inflationary trends. One of the key strategies has been the implementation of targeted subsidies on essential goods such as food, fuel, and medicine to help mitigate the impact of price increases on the most vulnerable populations (Daher et al., 2022). These subsidies, while costly, have been critical in ensuring access to basic necessities for both Lebanese citizens and Syrian refugees during periods of acute economic strain.

Additionally, efforts have been made to strengthen the social safety net through the expansion of cash assistance programmes. These programmes, often supported by international donors and implemented in partnership with UN agencies, provide direct financial support to families struggling to meet their basic needs, helping to cushion the impact of inflation on household budgets (Geha & Talhouk, 2019). By targeting assistance to those most in need, these initiatives aim to alleviate immediate financial pressures and prevent further deterioration into poverty.

Another important aspect of the policy response has been the focus on economic stabilization and growth. Measures such as monetary policy adjustments, efforts to attract foreign investment, and initiatives to support small and medium-sized enterprises have been pursued to stimulate economic activity and create employment opportunities (Saleh & Athari, 2023). These efforts are crucial for restoring economic confidence, promoting sustainable growth, and reducing the vulnerability of the economy to future shocks.

In parallel, international actions have also emphasized the need for structural reforms within Lebanon to address long-standing economic inefficiencies and governance issues. Conditional financial assistance and support packages have been linked to the implementation of reforms in areas such as public finance management, corruption reduction, and sectoral regulation. These reforms are intended to improve the overall economic governance in Lebanon, ensuring a more resilient and sustainable economic foundation moving forward.

The combined government and international actions represent a multifaceted approach to addressing the economic consequences of the Syrian refugee crisis in Lebanon. By focusing on both immediate relief measures and longer-term economic stabilization and reform efforts, these policy responses aim to mitigate the impact of inflation, support affected populations, and lay the groundwork for a more stable and prosperous future for all residents of Lebanon.

5.2 *Efficacy and Challenges*

The efficacy of the policy responses and mitigation strategies deployed to counter the economic fallout of the Syrian refugee crisis in Lebanon presents a complex picture, marked by both achievements and significant challenges. While these interventions have undoubtedly provided crucial support to vulnerable populations and contributed to some level of economic stabilization, their implementation has faced obstacles that highlight the intricate dynamics at play in Lebanon's socio-economic landscape.

One of the notable successes of the implemented policies has been the provision of immediate relief to those most in need. Subsidies on essential goods and cash assistance programmes have played critical roles in ensuring access to basic necessities for countless families, both Lebanese and refugees, amidst the inflationary pressures. These measures have acted as vital lifelines, preventing a deeper slide into poverty and food insecurity for many. Similarly, efforts to stimulate economic activity through support for small and medium-sized enterprises have shown promise in creating jobs and fostering economic resilience (Yacoub & Al Maalouf, 2023).

However, the challenges encountered in the implementation of these strategies have been multifaceted. The sustainability of subsidies, for example, has been a significant concern, given Lebanon's strained public finances. The reliance on external financial support for these subsidies and assistance programmes underscores the fragile fiscal situation and raises questions about long-term viability. Additionally, the targeting and distribution of aid have sometimes been hampered by inefficiencies and corruption, limiting the effectiveness of assistance programmes and undermining trust in public institutions.

The broader economic stabilization and reform efforts have also encountered hurdles. Structural reforms, critical for long-term economic recovery and governance improvement, have progressed slowly, hindered by political deadlock and resistance from entrenched interests opposed to change. This resistance has impeded the implementation of necessary reforms, such as those aimed at enhancing public finance management and reducing corruption, which are essential for attracting foreign investment and support.

Moreover, the coordination between Lebanese authorities, international donors, and NGOs has sometimes been fraught with challenges, affecting the efficiency and impact of response efforts (Kelley, 2017). Differences in priorities, bureaucratic obstacles, and logistical issues have occasionally slowed down the deployment of aid and the execution of projects designed to support economic recovery and infrastructure development.

5.3 *Recommendations for Policy Improvements*

To more effectively tackle the inflationary pressures and cost of living challenges exacerbated by the Syrian refugee crisis in Lebanon, a nuanced approach to policy improvement is crucial. Recommendations for enhancing existing measures focus on sustainability, inclusivity, and long-term economic resilience. A key area of improvement is the targeted and efficient deployment of subsidies and financial assistance. While these measures have provided essential relief, refining targeting mechanisms to ensure aid reaches the most vulnerable populations can enhance their impact. Implementing more sophisticated data collection and analysis methods to identify those in greatest need, while minimizing leakage and corruption, will improve the efficacy of these programmes.

Additionally, increasing the sustainability of financial assistance programmes through the integration of development-oriented goals is vital. Transitioning from short-term relief to long-term development assistance can help build economic resilience among affected populations. This involves linking cash assistance programmes to education, training, and employment opportunities, encouraging self-reliance and contributing to the broader economy. Such an approach not only addresses immediate needs but also fosters long-term economic integration and stability.

Investing in infrastructure and public services is another critical recommendation. The refugee influx has placed a significant strain on Lebanon's infrastructure and public services, exacerbating economic vulnerabilities. Enhancing public infrastructure, including water, sanitation, energy, and transportation systems, will improve the quality of life for all residents, support economic activity, and attract investment. This requires not only national investment but also international support and collaboration, leveraging both public and private sector resources.

Pursuing comprehensive structural reforms to address underlying economic and governance issues is essential for long-term stability. This includes reforms in public finance management, anti-corruption measures, and regulatory improvements to encourage business development and foreign investment. These reforms are challenging but necessary to create a more transparent, efficient, and resilient economic environment.

Finally, fostering regional cooperation and international partnerships is crucial for addressing the broader implications of the refugee crisis and its economic impacts. Collaborative efforts can mobilize additional resources, share best practices, and coordinate humanitarian and development assistance more effectively. Engaging with international organizations, neighbouring countries, and other stakeholders in a concerted effort to find sustainable solutions to the refugee crisis will benefit Lebanon and the region as a whole.

These recommendations emphasize the need for a holistic and coordinated approach to policy improvement, one that addresses immediate challenges while laying the groundwork for long-term economic and social stability. By focusing on sustainability, inclusivity, and resilience, Lebanon can better navigate the complex landscape of inflationary pressures and cost of living challenges, creating a more stable and prosperous future for all its residents.

6 Case Studies: Navigating Economic Hardship

In the face of Lebanon's inflationary pressures, individuals and communities have displayed remarkable resilience and adaptability, crafting innovative strategies to navigate the economic hardships. One compelling case study involves a community initiative in a Beirut neighbourhood, where residents have established a cooperative grocery store. By pooling resources and leveraging collective buying power, this cooperative has managed to secure food and essential goods at lower prices, directly combating the inflation that has made everyday items unaffordable for many. Such grassroots efforts not only provide immediate relief but also strengthen community bonds, fostering a sense of solidarity and mutual support in challenging times.

Another example of individual resilience is found in the story of a Lebanese teacher who, facing salary cuts and the rising cost of living, began offering online tutoring sessions to students internationally. This innovative approach not only supplemented her income but also connected her with a global community, illustrating how digital platforms can provide economic opportunities beyond local constraints. These cases reflect the broader trend of individuals and communities leveraging creativity and solidarity to withstand economic adversity, emphasizing the potential of collective action and digital innovation in facing inflationary challenges.

On the business front, Lebanese companies have also had to adapt to the inflationary environment, with many finding creative ways to manage increased costs and altered market dynamics. A notable example is a small manufacturing firm in Tripoli that responded to rising raw material costs by shifting towards the production of more cost-effective, locally sourced alternatives. This pivot not only allowed the firm to maintain competitive pricing but also stimulated local supply chains, contributing to the broader economic resilience. Additionally, several Lebanese start-ups have embraced digital transformation, adopting e-commerce models to reduce operational costs and reach a wider customer base. These digital strategies have opened new revenue streams and mitigated the impact of reduced physical sales, showcasing the role of innovation in business survival and growth amid economic challenges.

These case studies of individual and community responses, alongside business adaptations, highlight the multifaceted strategies employed to cope with Lebanon's inflationary pressures. They underscore the importance of innovation, solidarity, and adaptability in overcoming economic hardships, offering valuable lessons on resilience and ingenuity in the face of adversity.

7 Conclusion

The exploration of inflationary pressures and the cost of living challenges in Lebanon, set against the backdrop of the Syrian refugee crisis, reveals a complex tapestry of economic strain and resilience. This chapter has delved into the multifaceted impacts of the crisis, from the sector-specific inflations affecting housing, food, and services, to the broader economic implications for consumption patterns, poverty rates, and overall economic stability. Through the lens of policy responses and mitigation strategies, we've seen the efforts of both the Lebanese government and international bodies to navigate these challenges, alongside the remarkable adaptability of individuals, communities, and businesses in the face of adversity.

The critical evaluation of these responses and strategies, coupled with recommendations for policy improvements, underscores the necessity of a nuanced and comprehensive approach to addressing the economic fallout of the refugee crisis. The case studies presented illustrate not just the hardship and economic challenges but also the incredible capacity for innovation and resilience among the Lebanese people and Syrian refugees alike.

References

Baumann, H. (2021). The causes, nature, and effect of the current crisis of Lebanese capitalism. In *Power-sharing after civil war* (pp. 61–77). Routledge.

BouChabke, S., & Haddad, G. (2021). Ineffectiveness, poor coordination, and corruption in humanitarian aid: The Syrian refugee crisis in Lebanon. *Voluntas: International Journal of Voluntary and Nonprofit Organizations, 32*(4), 894–909.

Corriero, A. C., Aborode, A. T., Reggio, M., & Shatila, N. (2022). The impact of COVID-19 and the economic crisis on Lebanese public health: Food insecurity and healthcare disintegration. *Ethics, Medicine and Public Health, 24*, 100802.

Daher, B., Hamie, S., Pappas, K., & Roth, J. (2022). Examining Lebanon's resilience through a water-energy-food nexus lens. *Frontiers in Sustainable Food Systems, 6*, 748343.

Dahham, J., Kremer, I., Hiligsmann, M., Hamdan, K., Nassereddine, A., Evers, S. M., & Rizk, R. (2023). Valuation of costs in health economics during financial and economic crises: A case study from Lebanon. *Applied Health Economics and Health Policy, 21*(1), 31–38.

Elia, J., Al Maalouf, N. J., Sawaya, C., Al Khoury, C., Karam, M., & Zakhem, N. B. (2023). The vulnerability of Lebanese alpha banks to the macroeconomic downturn and stress testing. *Migration Letters, 20*(8), 92–110.

Geha, C., & Talhouk, J. (2019). From recipients of aid to shapers of policies: Conceptualizing government–United Nations relations during the Syrian refugee crisis in Lebanon. *Journal of Refugee Studies, 32*(4), 645–663.

Habib, R. R., Ziadee, M., Abi Younes, E., El Asmar, K., & Jawad, M. (2020). The association between living conditions and health among Syrian refugee children in informal tented settlements in Lebanon. *Journal of Public Health, 42*(3), e323–e333.

Jomaa, L., Nasreddine, L., Naja, F., Chehade, L., & Hwalla, N. (2021). Sustainable, healthy and affordable diets for children in Lebanon: A call for action in dire times. *Sustainability, 13*(23), 13245.

Jones, P. S. (2023). *Human rights and development*. Taylor & Francis.

Kelley, N. (2017). Responding to a refugee influx: Lessons from Lebanon. *Journal on Migration and Human Security, 5*(1), 82–104.

Khalil, S., & Dagher, D. (2024). From "Switzerland" to "Venezuela" of the Middle East: Who is harmed the most by inflation in Lebanon? *International Journal of Social Economics, 51*(1), 1–17.

Kharroubi, S., Naja, F., Diab-El-Harake, M., & Jomaa, L. (2021). Food insecurity pre-and post the COVID-19 pandemic and economic crisis in Lebanon: Prevalence and projections. *Nutrients, 13*(9), 2976.

Kikano, F., Fauveaud, G., & Lizarralde, G. (2021). Policies of exclusion: The case of Syrian refugees in Lebanon. *Journal of Refugee Studies, 34*(1), 422–452.

Marrouch, W., & Sayour, N. (2021). Hedonic housing prices and environmental quality in Lebanon. *International Journal of Housing Markets and Analysis, 14*(5), 953–968.

Saleh, A. M., & Athari, S. A. (2023). Examining the impact of entrepreneurial orientation on new venture performance in the emerging economy of Lebanon: A moderated mediation analysis. *Sustainability, 15*(15), 11982.

Sumpf, D., Isaila, V., & Najjar, K. (2016). *The impact of the Syria crisis on Lebanon* (pp. 269–308). Springer International Publishing.

Yacoub, L., & Al Maalouf, N. J. (2023). Resilience amidst Lebanese crisis: Analyzing human resource practices. *Migration Letters, 20*(8), 554–572.

CHAPTER 6

Trade Disruptions and Economic Realignments: Adapting to New Realities in Post-crisis Lebanon

1 Introduction

The profound economic tremors felt by Lebanon in the wake of the Syrian refugee crisis have precipitated a complex web of trade disruptions and realignments, marking a period of significant transformation for the nation's trade dynamics. The influx of over a million refugees has not only strained Lebanon's socio-economic fabric but also its traditional trade routes and partnerships, necessitating a re-evaluation of its economic strategies and international relations. This chapter delves into the intricate interplay between these disruptions and the subsequent shifts in trade patterns, underscoring the critical impact on Lebanon's economy.

Before the crisis, Lebanon enjoyed a dynamic trade environment, characterized by established routes and partnerships that facilitated a robust exchange of goods and services within the region and beyond (Chauffour, 2013). However, the onset of the Syrian conflict and the resulting refugee influx have disrupted these traditional trade dynamics, presenting both challenges and opportunities for the Lebanese economy. The alterations in import and export patterns have not only affected the balance of trade but also prompted the emergence of new economic partnerships, as the nation sought to mitigate the adverse effects and explore new markets (Dbouk, 2020).

This chapter aims to provide a comprehensive overview of these trade disruptions, analysing their implications for Lebanon's economic stability

M. Zreik, *The Syrian Refugee Crisis and Lebanon's Economic Landscape*, https://doi.org/10.1007/978-3-031-68471-5_6

and growth. It explores how the changing geopolitical landscape has forced a reconfiguration of trade routes and the formation of alternative partnerships. By examining the impact on local industries and the broader economy, the chapter sheds light on the resilience and adaptability of Lebanese businesses in the face of such unprecedented challenges.

This chapter highlights the human dimension of the crisis. Each narrative is backed by data on refugee demographics and living conditions, providing a personal lens through which theoretical concepts of displacement and human rights are explored. Moreover, the role of international aid and trade agreements emerges as a pivotal factor in this narrative, offering a lifeline to an economy grappling with the dual challenges of political instability and the pressures of hosting a large refugee population. This analysis seeks to evaluate the effectiveness of these interventions in stabilizing the trade sector and supporting economic recovery.

Through a combination of economic data, policy analysis, and case studies, this chapter paints a detailed picture of the trade disruptions caused by the Syrian refugee crisis and the strategic responses employed by Lebanon. It underscores the importance of adaptive strategies in overcoming the obstacles posed by such disruptions, aiming to provide valuable insights into the broader implications for economic policy and international cooperation in a post-crisis context.

2 Impact on Traditional Trade Routes

2.1 Pre-crisis Trade Dynamics

Before the onset of the Syrian crisis, Lebanon's trade landscape was a vibrant tableau, marked by its strategic position as a crossroads for commerce between the East and West (Zreik, 2021). This advantageous geographical location, coupled with a liberal economic policy, facilitated a thriving trade network that extended across the Mediterranean and beyond. Lebanon's ports, notably the Port of Beirut, served as pivotal hubs for maritime trade, connecting the country with key markets in Europe, the Middle East, and Asia (Arvis et al., 2018). This connectivity was further bolstered by Lebanon's historical and cultural ties with neighbouring countries, enabling a rich tapestry of trade relations that underpinned the nation's economic vitality (Nisan, 2017).

Lebanese exporters and importers leveraged these established routes to trade a diverse array of goods, from agricultural produce and textiles to machinery and consumer electronics. The country's trade partnerships were equally varied, encompassing a mix of traditional allies and emerging markets, each contributing to a dynamic economic ecosystem. These relationships were underpinned by a series of bilateral and multilateral trade agreements, which facilitated smoother exchange of goods and services, reduced tariffs, and encouraged foreign investment (Baroudi, 2005).

Moreover, Lebanon's economic landscape was characterized by its vibrant entrepreneurial spirit and a strong private sector, which played a critical role in navigating the global trade environment. The pre-crisis period saw Lebanese businesses expanding their reach, exploring new markets, and establishing Lebanon as a key player in regional trade (Elmustapha & Hoppe, 2020). The synergy between Lebanon's strategic location, its diversified trade partnerships, and the entrepreneurial prowess of its private sector fuelled economic growth and development, positioning the country as a vital commercial hub in the Middle East.

However, this thriving trade environment faced unforeseen challenges with the advent of the Syrian refugee crisis. The crisis not only strained Lebanon's socio-economic resources but also its trade dynamics. The disruption of traditional trade routes and the shift in regional geopolitical landscapes necessitated a re-evaluation of Lebanon's trade strategies. Yet, the pre-crisis trade dynamics laid a foundation of resilience, enabling Lebanon to navigate the complexities of a rapidly changing trade environment (Calì et al., 2015). These established routes and partnerships, though challenged, provided a framework within which Lebanon could begin to adapt and realign its trade strategies in response to the new realities imposed by the crisis.

2.2 *Disruptions and Shifts*

The Syrian refugee crisis, one of the most significant humanitarian events in recent history, has had a profound impact on Lebanon's trade dynamics, altering traditional trade routes and partnerships that have been the backbone of the country's economy. The influx of over a million refugees into Lebanon, a country with a population of just over six million, has placed immense pressure on its economic infrastructure, leading to significant shifts in import and export patterns (Dbouk, 2020). These shifts have necessitated a re-evaluation and adaptation of Lebanon's trade strategies to mitigate the adverse effects on its economy.

One of the immediate impacts of the crisis on Lebanon's trade dynamics was the disruption of land routes used for the transit of goods. The border closures and increased security measures significantly hindered the flow of trade between Lebanon and its traditional partners, particularly Syria, a key land bridge to other Arab markets (Mourad, 2019). This disruption forced Lebanese traders to seek alternative, often more expensive, routes for their goods, such as maritime transport, which increased the cost of trade and impacted the competitiveness of Lebanese products in international markets (Fakhoury, 2021).

Moreover, the crisis led to a shift in Lebanon's import patterns. The country saw an increased demand for consumer goods, medical supplies, and food products to meet the needs of the refugee population (Kelley, 2017). This shift not only affected the balance of trade but also put additional pressure on Lebanon's already strained public services and infrastructure. The increased demand for basic goods further exacerbated the economic challenges faced by the Lebanese population, leading to increased competition for limited resources and services (Baumann, 2021).

The refugee crisis also influenced Lebanon's export patterns. The disruption of traditional trade routes and the instability in neighbouring markets led to a decline in exports to traditional partners. Lebanese exporters faced challenges in accessing previously reliable markets, prompting a search for new markets outside the immediate region (Ahmad, 2020). This search was complicated by the fact that entering new markets often requires navigating different regulatory environments and establishing new trade relationships, which can be time-consuming and resource-intensive.

In response to these disruptions, Lebanon has witnessed the emergence of new economic partnerships and trade agreements. The country has sought to diversify its trade partners and explore new markets in Europe, Asia, and Africa (Austin et al., 2017). This strategic pivot aims to reduce Lebanon's dependency on its traditional trade routes and partners and mitigate the impact of regional instability on its economy. The process of forging new partnerships and entering new markets is challenging but essential for Lebanon's economic resilience in the face of ongoing crises.

Additionally, the crisis has prompted a re-evaluation of the role of international aid and trade agreements in supporting Lebanon's economy. International aid initiatives have played a crucial role in providing immediate relief to the refugee population and supporting Lebanon's public infrastructure (Kelley, 2017). However, the long-term sustainability of

Lebanon's economy depends on the effectiveness of trade agreements and economic support packages designed to facilitate access to new markets and promote economic growth.

3 Emergence of New Economic Partnerships

3.1 New Trade Partners

In the wake of the Syrian refugee crisis, Lebanon has found itself at a crossroads, facing significant trade disruptions that have compelled the country to explore new economic avenues. This challenging scenario has catalysed the emergence of new economic partnerships, marking a pivotal shift in Lebanon's trade dynamics. As traditional trade routes became untenable and previous partnerships were strained under the weight of geopolitical shifts, Lebanon began to cast its net wider, seeking alliances beyond its immediate neighbourhood. This strategic pivot was not merely a response to the crisis but a forward-looking approach to diversify its economic base and secure a more resilient future.

The formation of new trade partnerships has been instrumental in this process. With the Middle East region embroiled in instability, Lebanon turned its attention towards European, Asian, and African markets (Jaroudi & Hammoud, 2019). These new relationships are built on a foundation of mutual economic interests, with Lebanon offering a diverse range of exports from agricultural products to technological services. The appeal of Lebanese goods in these markets is bolstered by the country's reputation for quality and its strategic geographical position, which, despite regional turmoil, remains a significant advantage.

Europe has emerged as a particularly important partner in this new trade landscape. Agreements with European countries have opened up markets for Lebanese agricultural and manufactured goods, which are valued for their quality and authenticity (Mukahhal et al., 2022). These partnerships are supported by trade facilitation agreements and aid packages aimed at enhancing Lebanon's export capabilities and market access. Similarly, Asian markets have offered Lebanon new opportunities, particularly in the technology and service sectors, where Lebanese entrepreneurs are making inroads with innovative solutions and partnerships (Zreik, 2022).

The shift towards Africa represents a strategic exploration of markets with growing demand for Lebanese products and investment. African countries, with their burgeoning markets and need for infrastructure and expertise, present a unique opportunity for Lebanese businesses. These partnerships are not just trade-based but are increasingly characterized by investment in sectors such as telecommunications, banking, and construction, reflecting a deepening of economic ties (Atala et al., 2016).

These new economic partnerships are not without their challenges, including the need for Lebanon to adapt to different market regulations, standards, and consumer preferences. However, they represent a critical evolution in Lebanon's economic strategy, moving from reliance on traditional partners and routes to a more diversified and resilient trade portfolio. This diversification strategy, prompted by the crisis, is a testament to Lebanon's agility and its businesses' capacity to innovate and adapt. As Lebanon continues to navigate the complexities of its economic landscape, these new partnerships stand as pillars of hope, promising a more stable and prosperous future amidst ongoing uncertainties.

3.2 *Impact on Local Industries*

The emergence of new economic partnerships in the wake of the Syrian refugee crisis has had a transformative impact on Lebanon's local industries and economic sectors. As the country ventured into uncharted territories with new trade partners, these relationships have begun to reshape the landscape in which Lebanese industries operate. The adaptation to new markets and the diversification of trade relationships have provided both opportunities and challenges for local businesses, compelling them to innovate and adjust to the demands of a globalized market.

One of the most significant impacts has been on the agricultural sector. With Europe and certain African countries becoming new destinations for Lebanese products, farmers and producers have had to meet stricter quality standards and certifications. This adjustment has not only improved the competitiveness of Lebanese agricultural goods but has also spurred modernization within the sector, encouraging sustainable practices and the adoption of new technologies (Mukahhal et al., 2022). The opening of these new markets has provided a much-needed boost to the agriculture sector, which has traditionally been a cornerstone of Lebanon's economy but faced numerous challenges, including limited access to water and arable land (El Khansa, 2017).

The manufacturing sector, too, has felt the ripple effects of these new economic ties. Lebanese manufacturers, known for their craftsmanship in areas such as jewellery, fashion, and food processing, have found new avenues for export (Gordon, 2016). However, entering these markets has required adjustments in production processes, marketing strategies, and product designs to cater to different cultural tastes and standards. This evolution has driven innovation within the sector, pushing Lebanese manufacturers to elevate their products and engage with global trends more proactively (Kelley, 2017).

Moreover, the service industry, particularly information technology and financial services, has benefited from the expansion into Asian markets (DeQuero-Navarro et al., 2020). The demand for digital solutions and financial expertise in these regions has opened up new opportunities for Lebanese firms, highlighting the country's strength in knowledge-based industries. This shift towards services reflects a broader trend in Lebanon's economic adaptation, where high-value services are becoming increasingly crucial to the country's export portfolio.

Despite these positive developments, the transition has not been without its challenges. Local industries have had to navigate the complexities of entering new markets, including dealing with different regulatory environments, logistical challenges, and the need for market-specific knowledge. Additionally, the internal challenges posed by Lebanon's economic situation, including currency instability and infrastructural deficiencies, have added layers of complexity to this transition.

4 Challenges of Trade Adaptation

4.1 Adaptation Strategies

The adaptation to a significantly altered trade environment, precipitated by the Syrian refugee crisis and the emergence of new economic partnerships, has presented Lebanese businesses and industries with a set of formidable challenges. Navigating this new landscape has required a multifaceted approach, blending innovation, strategic planning, and resilience. Lebanese enterprises, both large and small, have employed a variety of strategies to adapt to these changes, demonstrating remarkable agility in the face of adversity.

One key strategy has been the diversification of markets and products. Faced with the disruption of traditional trade routes and the dynamics of new markets, Lebanese businesses have sought to broaden their horizons, exploring untapped markets and adjusting their product lines to meet diverse consumer demands (Dbouk, 2020). This diversification has not only helped mitigate the risks associated with dependency on a limited number of markets but has also spurred creativity and innovation, leading to the development of new products and services (Mourad, 2019).

Investment in technology and digital transformation has emerged as another crucial adaptation strategy. The digitalization of operations has enabled Lebanese companies to enhance their efficiency, improve their access to new markets, and better meet the expectations of a global customer base. From e-commerce platforms facilitating cross-border sales to digital marketing strategies aimed at reaching a wider audience, technology has played a pivotal role in Lebanon's trade adaptation efforts (Daza Jaller et al., 2020).

Moreover, Lebanese businesses have increasingly focused on enhancing their value proposition through quality improvement and certification. Recognizing the stringent standards of new markets, particularly in Europe and Asia, companies have invested in quality control, obtained international certifications, and embraced sustainable practices (Harb et al., 2021). These efforts have not only improved the competitiveness of Lebanese products but have also aligned local industries with global trends towards sustainability and corporate social responsibility.

Collaboration and networking have also been instrumental in Lebanon's trade adaptation process. Businesses have sought partnerships with local and international entities, including trade associations, export promotion agencies, and foreign investors, to leverage collective strengths and navigate the complexities of global trade (Nachum et al., 2023). These collaborations have facilitated knowledge exchange, opened up new business opportunities, and provided support in logistics and market entry strategies.

In adapting to the changed trade environment, Lebanese businesses have demonstrated a commendable level of resilience and resourcefulness. The strategies employed—ranging from market and product diversification to technological investment and strategic partnerships—reflect a proactive approach to overcoming the challenges posed by the new trade dynamics. While the path ahead remains fraught with uncertainties, the adaptability of Lebanon's business sector offers a beacon of hope for the country's economic recovery and growth.

4.2 *Barriers to Adaptation*

Adapting to new trade dynamics, precipitated by external shocks such as the Syrian refugee crisis and the consequent shift in economic partnerships, has presented Lebanese businesses and industries with a myriad of challenges and obstacles. While the shift towards new markets and the diversification of trade relations are essential for Lebanon's economic resilience, the journey is fraught with barriers that complicate this adaptation process. These challenges are not just external, tied to the global trade environment, but also internal, stemming from within Lebanon's economic and regulatory framework.

One of the primary barriers is the regulatory and logistical hurdles associated with entering new markets. Each new market comes with its own set of rules, standards, and consumer preferences, requiring businesses to navigate a complex web of regulations and customs procedures (El Jurdi & Houjeir, 2020). This can be particularly daunting for small and medium-sized enterprises (SMEs) that lack the resources and expertise to manage these requirements efficiently. Additionally, the logistical challenges of accessing distant markets, especially in the absence of direct trade routes, add to the cost and complexity of trade, diminishing the competitiveness of Lebanese products (Mukahhal et al., 2022).

Another significant challenge is the financial constraint. The economic instability in Lebanon, marked by currency devaluation and banking restrictions, has severely impacted businesses' ability to invest in necessary adaptations, whether it be technology, market research, or quality certifications. Access to financing remains a critical hurdle, with many Lebanese businesses struggling to secure the capital needed to pivot towards new opportunities or even sustain their operations in the face of increased operational costs (Gillespie & Swan, 2021).

Moreover, the internal political instability and infrastructural deficits further exacerbate the barriers to adaptation. Persistent political deadlock and governance issues have led to a lack of coherent economic policies and support mechanisms for businesses aiming to adapt to new trade dynamics. The inadequacy of infrastructure, notably in terms of electricity, telecommunications, and transportation, hinders operational efficiency and increases the cost of doing business in Lebanon, making it challenging for local industries to meet the demands of international markets.

The human capital aspect also presents a barrier. The need for new skills and knowledge to compete in global markets requires significant investment in workforce development and training. However, the brain drain phenomenon, with many skilled workers leaving the country in search of better opportunities, has depleted Lebanon's pool of human resources, making it difficult for businesses to adapt to the new demands of international trade (Dibeh et al., 2018).

In facing these barriers, Lebanese businesses and industries are navigating a tightrope, balancing the imperative to adapt against the backdrop of significant internal and external challenges. The path forward requires not only individual enterprise resilience but also concerted efforts at the national and international levels to address these systemic barriers and facilitate a smoother adaptation process for Lebanon's trade sector.

5 Role of International Aid and Trade Agreements

5.1 *International Aid Initiatives*

In the aftermath of the Syrian refugee crisis, international aid has played a pivotal role in supporting Lebanon's battered economy and trade sector. The influx of refugees placed an immense strain on Lebanon's infrastructure and public services, exacerbating existing economic challenges and creating new ones. In this context, international aid initiatives have been crucial in mitigating the immediate impacts of the crisis and laying the groundwork for economic recovery and stability.

International aid to Lebanon has come in various forms, including financial assistance, grants, and in-kind support, aimed at both alleviating the immediate needs of the refugee population and bolstering the Lebanese economy. This aid has been instrumental in supporting public services such as education, healthcare, and waste management, which faced unprecedented pressure due to the crisis (Carpi, 2023). By addressing these critical areas, international aid has helped stabilize the socio-economic environment, creating a more conducive atmosphere for business operations and trade.

Moreover, a significant portion of international aid has been directed towards economic support initiatives, designed to rejuvenate Lebanon's trade sector and stimulate economic growth. These initiatives include infrastructure development projects, such as the upgrading of port facilities and transportation networks, which are vital for enhancing Lebanon's trade capacity and efficiency (El-Anis, 2021). Additionally, international aid has supported the development of export-oriented industries, providing the necessary training, resources, and market access to enable Lebanese businesses to compete on the international stage (Ahmed & Brennan, 2019).

International aid has also played a key role in facilitating trade agreements and partnerships, acting as a bridge between Lebanon and potential trade partners. Through diplomatic channels and international organizations, aid providers have worked to open up new markets for Lebanese products, negotiate trade agreements, and attract foreign investment (Asderaki, 2021). This role of international aid as a facilitator of trade has been crucial in diversifying Lebanon's economic partnerships and reducing its vulnerability to regional instabilities.

Furthermore, international aid initiatives have focused on capacity building within Lebanon's trade sector, offering technical assistance and advisory services to government institutions and private sector entities. This support has been aimed at improving Lebanon's trade policies, regulatory framework, and customs procedures, making it easier for Lebanese businesses to engage in international trade. By enhancing the overall trade ecosystem, international aid has contributed to creating a more favourable environment for economic growth and development.

5.2 *Trade Agreements and Economic Support*

In the complex landscape of Lebanon's post-crisis economy, trade agreements and economic support mechanisms have emerged as crucial instruments for mitigating the disruptions caused by the Syrian refugee crisis and ensuing regional instability. These agreements, both new and existing, have served as vital lifelines, enabling Lebanon to maintain and expand its trade relations amidst challenging circumstances. The strategic importance of such agreements cannot be overstated, as they have provided much-needed economic stability and opened pathways for recovery and growth.

One of the key roles of trade agreements in this context has been to facilitate access to new markets and secure favourable terms for Lebanese exports. In response to the crisis, Lebanon has actively sought to negotiate and enter into trade agreements with countries outside its traditional sphere of economic influence. These new agreements have been instrumental in diversifying Lebanon's trade partners and reducing its reliance on volatile regional markets. By securing preferential access to markets in

Europe, Asia, and Africa, Lebanon has been able to tap into new demand for its products, from agricultural goods to manufactured items, thereby offsetting some of the losses from disrupted traditional trade routes (Carmignani & Kler, 2018).

Moreover, existing trade agreements have been revisited and strengthened to better serve Lebanon's changing economic needs. The European Union (EU), for instance, has been a key partner in this regard, offering not just market access but also technical and financial support to help Lebanese businesses comply with EU standards and regulations (Seeberg, 2018). This support has been critical in enabling Lebanese products to compete in the highly competitive EU market, thereby sustaining and even increasing export volumes in certain sectors.

In addition to facilitating trade, these agreements have often been accompanied by economic support measures designed to bolster Lebanon's trade infrastructure and capacity. Investments in port modernization, customs automation, and logistics networks have been part of broader economic support packages, aiming to enhance Lebanon's overall trade efficiency and attractiveness as a trading partner (Soh et al., 2021). Such improvements are essential for reducing the cost and time of trade, making Lebanese products more competitive on the global stage.

Furthermore, trade agreements have served as frameworks for economic cooperation and development assistance, linking trade with broader economic reforms and investment in key sectors. Through these agreements, Lebanon has accessed not only markets but also expertise and resources for economic modernization, including in areas such as renewable energy, digital transformation, and small and medium enterprise development (Ben Hassen, 2021). This holistic approach has been pivotal in addressing both the immediate trade disruptions and the underlying vulnerabilities of Lebanon's economy.

5.3 *Effectiveness and Limitations*

The effectiveness of international aid and trade agreements in mitigating Lebanon's trade challenges in the aftermath of the Syrian refugee crisis presents a nuanced picture, marked by both significant achievements and notable limitations. These mechanisms have been instrumental in providing Lebanon with the necessary support to navigate through economic disruptions, yet their impact has been tempered by a range of structural and external challenges that persist within the country's economic landscape.

International aid and trade agreements have undoubtedly played a critical role in stabilizing Lebanon's economy during a period of unprecedented strain. Aid initiatives have bolstered public services and infrastructure, directly supporting the socio-economic conditions necessary for trade. Furthermore, trade agreements have opened up new markets for Lebanese products, offering a lifeline for businesses struggling with the loss of traditional trade routes. The support for infrastructure development, particularly in transportation and logistics, has enhanced Lebanon's trade capacity, reducing the cost and increasing the efficiency of exports. These efforts have provided a much-needed boost to Lebanon's trade sector, enabling it to maintain a level of activity despite the surrounding turmoil.

However, the effectiveness of these interventions has been constrained by several factors. One major limitation is the pervasive political and economic instability within Lebanon, which undermines the potential benefits of international aid and trade agreements. The frequent political deadlock and lack of effective governance have impeded the implementation of reforms and projects funded by international aid, delaying their impact on the economy. Additionally, Lebanon's deep-seated economic challenges, including high levels of debt and structural deficiencies, limit the ability of international support to effectuate lasting change without comprehensive internal reforms.

Another limitation is the mismatch between the immediate relief provided by international aid and the long-term developmental needs of Lebanon's trade sector. While aid has been crucial in addressing immediate needs, it has sometimes fallen short in fostering sustainable economic growth and trade capacity development (Verme et al., 2015). This is partly due to the short-term focus of some aid programmes, which do not always align with the longer-term strategic needs of Lebanon's economy, including investment in human capital, innovation, and diversification.

Moreover, the effectiveness of trade agreements in opening new markets for Lebanese products is often hampered by non-tariff barriers, such as stringent quality standards and regulatory requirements in target markets (Fuenfzig et al., 2021). While these agreements facilitate access, Lebanese businesses frequently face challenges in meeting these requirements, highlighting the need for further support in capacity building and standards compliance.

6 Case Studies: Industry-Specific Impacts and Responses

6.1 Agricultural Sector Response

The agricultural sector in Lebanon, pivotal to the country's economy and the livelihoods of its rural population, has faced considerable challenges in the wake of trade disruptions caused by regional instability and the Syrian refugee crisis (Mukahhal et al., 2022). These disruptions have necessitated a significant adaptation process within the sector, which has been characterized by resilience and innovation in the face of adversity. The response of the agricultural sector to these challenges provides a compelling case study of adaptation to new market realities.

Initially, the closure of traditional land routes due to the crisis severely impacted the export of agricultural products, particularly to Gulf Cooperation Council (GCC) countries, which were major destinations for Lebanese produce (Calì et al., 2015). This situation compelled the agricultural sector to look for alternative markets and develop new logistics solutions. One notable adaptation strategy was the shift towards maritime routes, despite their higher costs, to ensure the continuity of exports. This pivot not only demonstrated the sector's resilience but also its capacity to adjust to logistical challenges rapidly (Salameh & Chedid, 2020).

Furthermore, the sector has witnessed a significant push towards diversification of crops and adoption of sustainable agricultural practices. Recognizing the need to cater to the demands of new markets in Europe and beyond, Lebanese farmers have increasingly focused on high-value crops that meet international quality standards. This shift has been supported by international aid programmes aimed at enhancing agricultural productivity and sustainability, through the provision of training, improved seeds, and modern irrigation techniques (Mawad & Makki, 2023).

Moreover, the agricultural sector has embraced technology and innovation to overcome some of the challenges posed by the crisis. Digital platforms for marketing and sales have become increasingly popular among farmers, enabling them to reach new customers and markets without the need for traditional distribution channels (Abou-Najem et al., 2019). This digital transformation has not only opened up new avenues for sales but also improved the sector's resilience to future disruptions.

6.2 *Manufacturing Sector Response*

The manufacturing sector in Lebanon, known for its diverse output ranging from food products to industrial goods, has been compelled to undergo significant adjustments in response to the shifts in trade dynamics and the emergence of new economic partnerships. The sector's agility in adapting to these changes is a testament to its resilience and innovative spirit, faced with the dual challenges of regional instability and global market demands.

One of the most notable adjustments within the manufacturing sector has been the strategic pivot towards new markets. With traditional markets in the Middle East becoming less accessible due to the crisis, Lebanese manufacturers have turned their sights towards Europe, Asia, and Africa (Chatty, 2017). This shift required not only logistical adjustments but also adaptations in product specifications to meet different regulatory standards and consumer preferences. Manufacturers have invested in upgrading their production processes, obtaining international certifications, and ensuring compliance with the stringent quality standards of these new markets (Nassereddine & Wehbe, 2018).

Furthermore, the sector has embraced technological innovation to enhance its competitiveness. This includes the adoption of advanced manufacturing technologies, such as automation and digital manufacturing, to increase efficiency, reduce costs, and improve product quality. These technological advancements have enabled Lebanese manufacturers to maintain their edge in a highly competitive global market, despite the challenges posed by economic instability at home (Salameh, 2021).

Collaboration has also been a key theme in the sector's response to trade changes. Recognizing the benefits of collective action, manufacturers have engaged in partnerships with each other, with government bodies, and with international organizations to access new markets, participate in trade fairs, and benefit from shared logistics and marketing efforts. These collaborative efforts have been crucial in overcoming the barriers to market entry and in leveraging the strengths of Lebanon's manufacturing sector on the global stage.

7 Conclusion

The exploration of trade disruptions and subsequent economic realignments in Lebanon, in the wake of the Syrian refugee crisis, underscores a complex narrative of challenge and resilience. Lebanon's economy, particularly its trade dynamics, has undergone profound transformations, navigating through the upheaval of traditional trade routes, the forging of new economic partnerships, and the relentless pursuit of adaptation across various sectors. This chapter has illuminated not only the stark challenges faced by Lebanon but also the strategic responses that have emerged, highlighting a journey of adaptation and resilience.

The agricultural and manufacturing sectors, emblematic of the broader economic landscape, have demonstrated remarkable agility in responding to the shifts in trade dynamics. Their ability to diversify, innovate, and forge new paths in the face of adversity encapsulates the broader theme of this chapter: the capacity for resilience and strategic adaptation in the face of daunting challenges. The role of international aid and trade agreements has been pivotal, offering a lifeline and facilitating Lebanon's engagement with new markets, yet the journey is far from complete. These mechanisms, while crucial, intersect with a tapestry of internal and external challenges that continue to shape Lebanon's economic trajectory.

As Lebanon continues to navigate these turbulent waters, the lessons drawn from its experience are invaluable. They speak to the importance of flexibility, innovation, and international cooperation in overcoming trade disruptions. Moreover, they underscore the necessity of internal reforms and stable governance as foundational to leveraging international support effectively. The path forward for Lebanon is fraught with uncertainties, but the strategies employed and the resilience demonstrated offer a blueprint for navigating the complexities of global trade in the face of crisis.

References

Abou-Najem, S., Palacios-Rodríguez, G., Darwish, T., Faour, G., Kattar, S., Clavero Rumbao, I., & Navarro-Cerrillo, R. M. (2019). Land capability for agriculture, Hermel District, Lebanon. *Journal of Maps, 15*(2), 122–130.

Ahmad, A. (2020). *Distributed power generation for Lebanon: Market assessment and policy pathways.* World Bank.

Ahmed, F. U., & Brennan, L. (2019). An institution-based view of firms' early internationalization: Effectiveness of national export promotion policies. *International Marketing Review, 36*(6), 911–954.

Arvis, J. F., Vesin, V., Carruthers, R., & Ducruet, C. (2018). *Maritime networks, port efficiency, and hinterland connectivity in the Mediterranean*. World Bank Publications.

Asderaki, F. (2021). The EU in the Eastern Mediterranean: Multilateral and Bilateral Relations. In *The New Eastern Mediterranean Transformed: Emerging Issues and New Actors* (pp. 31–67). Springer International Publishing.

Atala, I., Dagher, W., & Chebib, N. (2016). Foreign direct investment in Lebanon. *International Journal of Economy, Management and Social Sciences, 5*(3), 39–51.

Austin, G., Dávila, C., & Jones, G. (2017). The alternative business history: Business in emerging markets. *Business history review, 91*(3), 537–569.

Baroudi, S. E. (2005). Lebanon's foreign trade relations in the postwar era: Scenarios for integration (1990–present). *Middle Eastern Studies, 41*(2), 201–225.

Baumann, H. (2021). The causes, nature, and effect of the current crisis of Lebanese capitalism. In *Power-Sharing after Civil War* (pp. 61–77). Routledge.

Ben Hassen, T. (2021). The state of the knowledge-based economy in the Arab world: Cases of Qatar and Lebanon. *EuroMed Journal of Business, 16*(2), 129–153.

Calì, M., Harake, W., Hassan, F., & Struck, C. (2015). *The impact of the Syrian conflict on Lebanese trade*. World Bank Publications.

Carmignani, F., & Kler, P. (2018). Your war, my problem: How conflict in a neighbour country hurts domestic development. *Economic Modelling, 70*, 484–495.

Carpi, E. (2023). *The Politics of Crisis-making: Forced Displacement and Cultures of Assistance in Lebanon*. Indiana University Press.

Chatty, D. (2017). The Syrian humanitarian disaster: Understanding perceptions and aspirations in Jordan, Lebanon and Turkey. *Global Policy, 8*, 25–32.

Chauffour, J. P. (2013). *From political to economic awakening in the Arab world: The path of economic integration*. World Bank Publications.

Daza Jaller, L., Gaillard, S., & Molinuevo, M. (2020). *The regulation of Digital Trade: Key policies and international trends*. World Bank Publications.

Dbouk, M. (2020). *Evolution and prospects of the economy of Lebanon*. Doctoral dissertation, Politecnico di Torino.

DeQuero-Navarro, B., Aoun Barakat, K., Shultz, C. J., Araque-Padilla, R. A., & Montero-Simo, M. J. (2020). From conflict to cooperation: A macromarketing view of sustainable and inclusive development in Lebanon and the Middle East. *Environmental Management, 66*, 232–247.

Dibeh, G., Fakih, A., & Marrouch, W. (2018). Decision to emigrate amongst the youth in Lebanon. *International Migration, 56*(1), 5–22.

El Jurdi, H., & Houjeir, R. (2020). Cultural norms and the marketplace: Favor economies in the Arab world. *Journal of Consumer Marketing, 37*(2), 226–235.

El Khansa, M. (2017). *Finding pathways for enhancing irrigated farming systems in Lebanon*. Doctoral dissertation, Université Montpellier.

El-Anis, I. (2021). Transport infrastructure and regional integration in the Middle East. *The Muslim World, 111*(1), 27–53.

Elmustapha, H., & Hoppe, T. (2020). Challenges and opportunities of business models in sustainable transitions: Evidence from solar energy niche development in Lebanon. *Energies, 13*(3), 670.

Fakhoury, T. (2021). Refugee return and fragmented governance in the host state: Displaced Syrians in the face of Lebanon's divided politics. *Third World Quarterly, 42*(1), 162–180.

Fuenfzig, M., Maggi, P., Besseling, C., Winkel, A., Flickenschild, M., Kowalski, P., Sidło, K., Malinowska, A., Peda, M., Hartwell, C., Augier, P., & Kamergi, N. (2021). *Ex-post evaluation of the impact of trade chapters of the Euro-Mediterranean Association Agreements with six partners: Algeria, Egypt, Jordan, Lebanon, Morocco and Tunisia*. Doctoral dissertation, European Commission-DG Research.

Gillespie, K., & Swan, K. S. (2021). *Global marketing*. Routledge.

Gordon, D. C. (2016). *The Republic of Lebanon: Nation in jeopardy*. Routledge.

Harb, W., Zaydan, R., & Vieira, M. (2021). Improving environmental performance in wine production by life cycle assessment: Case of Lebanese wine. *The International Journal of Life Cycle Assessment, 26*, 1146–1159.

Jaroudi, H., & Hammoud, M. S. (2019). Business leadership strategies under tenuous economic conditions. *International Journal of Applied Management Science, 11*(4), 314–332.

Kelley, N. (2017). Responding to a refugee influx: Lessons from Lebanon. *Journal on Migration and Human Security, 5*(1), 82–104.

Mawad, J. L., & Makki, M. (2023). Reflections on the initiatives of NGOs, INGOs, and UN organizations in eradicating poverty in Lebanon through the case study of RMF. *Arab Economic and Business Journal, 15*(2), 3.

Mourad, L. (2019). *Open borders, local closures: Decentralization and the politics of local responses to the Syrian refugee influx in Lebanon*. Doctoral dissertation, University of Toronto.

Mukahhal, W., Abebe, G. K., & Bahn, R. A. (2022). Opportunities and challenges for lebanese horticultural producers linked to corporate buyers. *Agriculture, 12*(5), 578.

Nachum, L., Stevens, C. E., Newenham-Kahindi, A., Lundan, S., Rose, E. L., & Wantchekon, L. (2023). Africa rising: Opportunities for advancing theory on people, institutions, and the nation state in international business. *Journal of International Business Studies, 54*(5), 938–955.

Nassereddine, A., & Wehbe, A. (2018). Competition and resilience: Lean manufacturing in the plastic industry in Lebanon. *Arab Economic and Business Journal, 13*(2), 179–189.

Nisan, M. (2017). *Politics and war in Lebanon: Unraveling the enigma*. Routledge.

Salameh, E. (2021). *Digital transformation: Readiness of the Lebanese manufacturing industry*. Doctoral dissertation, Notre Dame University-Louaize.

Salameh, R., & Chedid, R. (2020). Economic and geopolitical implications of natural gas export from the East Mediterranean: The case of Lebanon. *Energy Policy, 140*, 111369.

Seeberg, P. (2018). EU policies concerning Lebanon and the bilateral cooperation on migration and security–new challenges calling for new institutional practices? *Palgrave Communications, 4*(1), 1–9.

Soh, K. L., Wong, W. P., & Tang, C. F. (2021). The role of institutions at the nexus of logistic performance and foreign direct investment in Asia. *The Asian Journal of Shipping and Logistics, 37*(2), 165–173.

Verme, P., Gigliarano, C., Wieser, C., Hedlund, K., Petzoldt, M., & Santacroce, M. (2015). *The welfare of Syrian refugees: Evidence from Jordan and Lebanon*. World Bank Publications.

Zreik, M. (2021). The potential of a Sino-Lebanese partnership through the belt and road initiative (BRI). *Contemporary Arab Affairs, 14*(3), 125–145.

Zreik, M. (2022). The Chinese presence in the Arab region: Lebanon at the heart of the Belt and Road Initiative. *International Journal of Business and Systems Research, 16*(5–6), 644–662.

CHAPTER 7

Evaluating Lebanon's Economic Policy Response to the Syrian Refugee Crisis: Challenges and Alternatives

1 Introduction

The influx of Syrian refugees has presented Lebanon with a complex economic dilemma. Lebanon's economy was highly dependent on the service sector—especially banking and tourism—prior to the crisis, had insufficient industrial diversification, and had substantial public debt (Ben Hassen, 2021). These already fragile conditions have been further exacerbated by the flood of refugees. The stress on government resources was one of the most pressing problems. The United Nations High Commissioner for Refugees (UNHCR) has registered roughly 1.5 million Syrian refugees in Lebanon (Janmyr, 2022). This has placed additional strain on Lebanon's already overburdened public utilities.

Demand for essential services such as healthcare, education, electricity, and trash management has skyrocketed in response to the sudden increase in the population, bringing some places to the verge of collapse (David et al., 2020). Additionally, the housing market has been saturated, leading in rental price inflation which, in turn, influences the cost of living for the entire population (Nseir, 2022). An inflow of low-skilled workers has boosted competition for jobs and further complicated an already difficult labour market. As a result, incomes have fallen and unemployment and underemployment have become even more widespread in Lebanon. The government's fiscal position has worsened as a result of the growth of the informal economy.

M. Zreik, *The Syrian Refugee Crisis and Lebanon's Economic Landscape*, https://doi.org/10.1007/978-3-031-68471-5_7

Not only have vital land routes through Syria been closed, but the conflict has also caused a reorientation of commercial partnerships, which has affected trade (De Groot et al., 2022). This has had far-reaching effects on Lebanon's trade balance, necessitating a deliberate re-evaluation of trade ties and pathways. The World Bank predicts that Lebanon's economy will decrease in the years after the crisis due to the cumulative effect of these problems on GDP (Kharroubi et al., 2021).

With little help from abroad, fiscal policy has struggled to keep up with the rising price of housing refugees. The Lebanese government has had to strike a balance between increasing expenditure to help refugees and keeping up with infrastructure and the need to keep public debt from ballooning out of control. Policy solutions in Lebanon have been rendered more complicated by the country's fragile social and political fabric, calling for careful negotiation and consensus-building across varied political and sectarian interests.

Lebanon's society and government have been put to the test by the refugee crisis, which has already strained economic systems. Because of the complexity of the interplay between the economy and broader political and social issues, formulating effective policy responses is difficult (Fakhoury & Stel, 2023). Without a resolution to the Syrian conflict, Lebanon's economy would continue to suffer, necessitating continuous and flexible governmental initiatives.

To alleviate short-term financial crisis and lay the groundwork for long-term economic recovery and stability, the effectiveness of policy reaction during economic crises is vital. When the economy is in a slump, the right policy moves can operate as stabilizers to lessen or heighten the impact of the downturn. These policies, which frequently include monetary and fiscal measures, intend to fix liquidity shortages, restore investor confidence, and provide safety nets for vulnerable populations.

By affecting the money supply and interest rates, monetary policy is crucial in stabilizing the economy during times of crisis. In order to stimulate lending and investment, central banks can take unorthodox measures, such as quantitative easing, to inject money into the economy (Rostagno et al., 2021). For instance, in order to stabilize financial markets and stimulate economic activity during the 2008–2009 global financial crisis, major central banks around the world lowered interest rates to record lows and bought massive amounts of financial assets (Tooze, 2018).

Government spending and taxation, known as fiscal policy, are just as important. To combat a recession and stimulate the economy, governments frequently increase expenditure during times of crisis, despite the resulting increase in deficits. Infrastructure spending, unemployment insurance, and other forms of direct aid to industries particularly hard hit by the recession are all possibilities. Providing tax relief is another way to put more money in the hands of people and companies for consumption and investment. When the Great Recession hit in 2009, the U.S. government used fiscal stimulus in the form of the American Recovery and Reinvestment Act (Klein & Staal, 2017).

The stability of financial institutions and markets depends on effective regulatory and structural policies. Restoring trust and avoiding potentially disastrous risk-taking are two benefits of tightening regulatory regimes. In addition, bailouts of essential industries or financial institutions may be part of the policy response in times of crisis in order to avert systemic collapse.

It is crucial that these policy responses be timed and coordinated with one another. Recessions can deepen and recoveries can drag out longer if actions are delayed or are insufficient, and double-dip recessions can occur if support is withdrawn too soon. Timely and well-coordinated policy measures are stressed frequently by the International Monetary Fund (IMF) and the World Bank (Ray et al., 2023).

The response to policy also includes an equitable dimension. In times of crisis, those who are already weakest in society tend to suffer the most. To safeguard vulnerable populations, social safety nets, job training programmes, and economic support are needed for the lowest-income households.

In this chapter, long-term strategies for both Lebanon and the international community are discussed. It includes detailed plans and policy recommendations, supported by economic forecasts and social theories on integration and resilience, aiming to provide a roadmap for sustainable development and social harmony.

2 Analysis of Monetary Policies

The effects of central bank interventions on inflation and currency stability are common focal points of monetary policy analysis in times of economic turmoil. To keep the economy stable, central banks use a variety of tools, the most important of which are the control of interest rates and the monetary supply. Inflation rates and currency stability are important measures of economic health, and both are affected by these policies (Ha et al., 2019).

Manipulating interest rates is a common practise in monetary policy. The goal of cutting interest rates is to increase spending and investment by making borrowing money cheaper (Furman & Summers, 2019). However, by limiting expenditure and borrowing, higher rates can help keep inflation in check (Iacoviello, 2005). But, the success of interest rate changes depends greatly on the state of the economy and the receptivity of financial institutions and customers to these shifts.

When conventional monetary policy options are exhausted, like when interest rates approach zero, a central bank may resort to quantitative easing. Central banks directly pump liquidity into the economy by acquiring huge quantities of financial assets, mainly government securities (Herbst et al., 2014). As a result, this measure can strengthen financial markets, reduce borrowing costs, and increase lending. The effect on inflation is potentially two-fold: it may assist prevent deflation in a sluggish economy, or it may lead to an overexpansion of the money supply and inflationary pressures if employed incorrectly.

The effects on the value of the currency are complex as well. Currency devaluation, increased import prices, and possible inflation may result from central bank measures that raise the money supply without a matching increase in economic activity. Currencies can be bolstered by policies that boost consumer and investor confidence. The European Central Bank's promise to do "whatever it takes" to protect the euro helped stabilize the currency during the region's debt crisis (Rostagno et al., 2021).

In addition, governments can manipulate their currency's value by intervening in the foreign exchange market. Such actions can be used to combat undesirable volatility or speculative attacks on a currency. Inflation is affected indirectly since a stronger currency makes imported goods cheaper, whereas a weaker currency makes them more expensive.

Understanding the time lag caused by monetary measures is crucial. The effects of a central bank's decisions on the economy may not become apparent for months or even years. Moreover, these interventions must be properly calibrated, as the global financial system's interconnected nature means that actions in one country can have considerable spillover effects on others.

There are many factors to consider when weighing the pros and cons of different monetary policy responses to the refugee crisis. Central banks are frequently in the front lines of changing policy in response to unexpected surges in population. Inflationary pressures on the host economy, strained governmental finances, and currency market volatility are all possible outcomes of such crises.

Monetary policy in nations that take in large numbers of refugees must deal with the immediate inflationary pressures caused by the increased demand for goods and services. Increased demand for goods and services from a growing populace can outstrip the economy's capacity to produce them, driving increasing costs (Klein & Pettis, 2020). To counteract rising prices, central banks may raise interest rates and tighten monetary policy. However, the potential for this move to stifle economic growth and increase the burden of debt repayment for both public and private debtors needs to be considered.

Furthermore, central banks should think about how this may affect the job market. Refugees may increase the available workforce, which may lead to lower salaries (Brell et al., 2020). An inflation-reducing effect from a surge in the labour supply may prompt central banks to relax monetary policy in an effort to boost investment and consumer spending.

The impact on the value of other currencies should also be taken into account. The immediate effect is likely to be a boost in demand for the local currency to purchase goods and services, as refugees rarely bring large financial capital with them. In order to keep the currency from appreciating too much and hurting export competitiveness, the central bank may decide to interfere in the foreign exchange markets. The results, however, can vary greatly in the long run. Assimilation of refugees into the economy can raise productivity and consumption rates, which, in turn, can stimulate GDP (Kancs & Lecca, 2018). By keeping credit available and inflation under control, a well-tuned monetary policy helps ease the process of integration.

Such monetary policy modifications must be evaluated in the context of the macroeconomy as a whole. A high debt-to-GDP ratio, for instance, might leave the central bank with little room to manoeuvre without jeopardizing government creditworthiness (Kaplan, 2016). To ensure that economic adjustments can be maintained in such a situation, monetary policymakers will need to strike a delicate balance with fiscal policy. A credible central bank is also essential in these circumstances. A central bank's capacity to manage expectations and keep the public confident in its commitment to monetary stability hinges on its ability to effectively communicate the rationale behind policy moves (Blinder et al., 2008).

3 Fiscal Adjustments and Their Impacts

3.1 Changes in Government Spending and Taxation

In the wake of a crisis, especially one with strong humanitarian components like an inflow of refugees, fiscal adjustments present a number of difficulties and possibilities. These modifications typically involve shifts in government expenditure and taxation, two potent instruments for countering economic upheavals and aiding vulnerable populations.

The urgent growth of public expenditures to meet the housing, healthcare, education, and social service needs of refugees may be necessary in the context of increased government spending brought on by a crisis. In addition to meeting immediate humanitarian needs, this fiscal reaction can stimulate the economy by increasing aggregate demand and bolstering the creation of new jobs (Kelley, 2017). However, larger fiscal deficits may result from this spending rise, which could necessitate more borrowing and, consequently, higher taxes or reductions in other government spending in the future.

When it comes to taxes, governments may decide to make changes to their policies during times of crisis. Either new taxes would have to be implemented to cover the cost of the extra spending, or temporary tax cuts for firms and individuals may be implemented to boost economic activity. Policymakers must evaluate the immediate benefits of tax reductions to stimulate the economy against the long-term necessity for a sustainable revenue base to pay public spending. Furthermore, the effect of fiscal adjustments is highly dependent on their design. Increases in spending can have a multiplier effect on the economy if they are allocated to areas with high employment elasticity or those that help build human capital, such education and training (Yen et al., 2015). If taxes are progressive, they will have less of an impact on the poor, who are typically the worst hit during economic downturns (Stiglitz, 2015).

Government spending increases and tax reform are two sides of the same coin. The immediate effects of a crisis can be mitigated, and the longer-term integration of refugees into the host economy can be supported, through the expansion of public services and the provision of social safety nets. However, the fiscal flexibility to do so is typically constricted, particularly in economies currently suffering fiscal imbalances. Future economic stability is at risk from rising public debt, which must be controlled wisely. Reforms to boost the effectiveness of public expenditure, boost tax compliance, and extend the tax base are generally necessary to complement fiscal adjustments and reduce these risks (Imam & Jacobs, 2014). While still addressing the immediate issues faced by a crisis, such measures can help to guarantee that fiscal policy remains on a sustainable path.

3.2 Evaluation of Fiscal Policies Aimed at Economic Stabilization

Assessing the efficacy, efficiency, and impact of economic stabilization fiscal measures on both the short- and long-term recovery and fiscal health is essential. These measures are implemented after major economic disruptions have occurred, such as a financial crisis, natural disaster, or a substantial influx of refugees. Effective fiscal policies aiming at economic stabilization generally involve countercyclical measures such as increased government investment on infrastructure projects, which can offer immediate employment while also laying the framework for long-term economic growth (Harting, 2021). In a similar vein, strengthening social safety nets to cushion the most vulnerable can keep spending steady and keep the economy from plunging further.

The evaluation also has to take fiscal policy efficiency into account. This relates to how quickly and accurately the fiscal stimulus is implemented. The objective is to channel funding towards areas with the most potential for a beneficial multiplier effect on economic activity. Low levels of waste and the diversion of resources away from their intended purposes are also hallmarks of efficient operations.

Several macroeconomic indicators help evaluate the effectiveness of fiscal measures in achieving economic stability. Indicators such as GDP growth, unemployment rates, and consumer spending levels can provide insight into the efficacy of government spending and tax policies (Chan et al., 2017). A decrease in the unemployment rate, for instance, after an increase in government spending could be indicative of successful policy implementation.

There are, of course, drawbacks to implementing fiscal policies. Increased public debt levels, for instance, could lead to higher interest rates and discourage private investment if expansionary fiscal policies are implemented (Traum & Yang, 2015). Therefore, the long-term viability of fiscal measures should also be factored into any assessment. Long-term stabilization frequently necessitates that fiscal growth is followed by consolidation phases, where government expenditure is reduced, and attempts are made to boost revenue, hence reducing public debt levels (Haffert & Mehrtens, 2015).

The distributional impacts of fiscal policy must to be factored into any assessment. Despite their common goal, initiatives to stabilize the economy may have varying effects on different demographics. For example, tax cuts could benefit higher-income individuals more than the lower-income groups if they are not structured to be progressive (Cansunar, 2021). Therefore, it is essential to evaluate whether fiscal policies are fair and help those who need it the most when the economy is in a slump. Finally, the broader policy environment, including monetary policy and structural reforms, might affect how effective fiscal policies are in achieving economic stabilization. When responding to an economic crisis, fiscal policies are most effective when they are part of a comprehensive policy response.

3.3 Consequences of Fiscal Adjustments on Public Services and Infrastructure

Public services and infrastructure may suffer greatly if budgets are rearranged. These corrections, which often involve a combination of spending cuts and tax increases, are enacted to restore fiscal balance and stabilize the economy. The provision of public services and the condition of infrastructure may be adversely affected by unexpected effects.

Public services including healthcare, education, and public safety may see budget cuts when government spending is reduced as part of fiscal adjustment (Herwartz & Theilen, 2021). The quality and availability of these vital services may suffer as a result of budget cuts. Longer wait times for treatment, lower availability of medical supplies, and a lack of healthcare experts are only some of the potential outcomes of budget cuts in the healthcare sector. The quality of education and the growth of human capital over time could be negatively impacted by budget cuts that result in higher class sizes, fewer resources for schools, and fewer extracurricular and support programmes.

In addition, when funds are scarce, infrastructure projects may be put on hold or even scrapped altogether. Decreased investment in infrastructure can have negative effects on economic growth due to the deterioration of roads, bridges, and public transit networks (Deng, 2013). When infrastructure is subpar, it reduces productivity, drives up prices, and sometimes even discourages domestic and international investment.

It's also crucial to remember that people don't necessarily feel the effects of budget cuts in the same ways. As they are more reliant on public services and have less resilience to their decline, low-income and marginalized populations often bear a disproportionate part of the burden. When public services fail, more affluent people may seek out private alternatives, but those with fewer financial resources may not have the same choice. In addition, cutting back on public services and infrastructure spending might have unintended implications that undermine the budget. If essential services are underfunded, it can have far-reaching social and economic consequences. Infrastructural breakdowns, for instance, can become far more expensive to fix if regular maintenance is neglected. Similarly, less investment in preventative healthcare might lead to increased healthcare expenses in the long term due to an increase in chronic diseases and emergency health crises.

4 Labour Market Regulations and Reforms

4.1 *Overview of Labour Market Challenges in the Wake of the Refugee Influx*

When countries already experiencing economic hardships take in a large number of refugees, the strain on their labour markets can be severe. Countries like Lebanon, which took in many Syrian refugees in the wake of the crisis, had to deal with a rapid influx of workers into the job market (Turner, 2015). This might lead to many severe implications that demand appropriate policy responses and reforms. The most pressing issue right now is the prospect of increasing competition for jobs, particularly in fields where refugees can readily assimilate due to lower skill requirements. Wages may fall as a result of increased competition, especially in unregulated, informal markets. Because local workers typically view migrants as a danger to their economic security, this effect can intensify tensions between the refugee population and the host society (Jacobsen, 2002).

In addition, the refugee population may change the equilibrium between supply and demand in the labour market, which could cause imbalances. Refugees may face underemployment and inefficient use of the labour force if their skills do not match those in demand in the host country. On the other hand, there may be industries that may use the abilities that migrants bring but are unable to fully profit from them due to regulatory restrictions and recognition of qualifications concerns.

Additionally, as refugees may have difficulty gaining regular employment due to legal and other impediments, the informal sector generally grows in response to an inflow of refugees. This can undercut labour market laws and lead to inferior working conditions, which affects both refugees and citizens (Arnholtz & Lillie, 2023). In addition to threatening the strength of the labour market's overall regulatory structure, the expansion of the informal sector can cause large losses in government revenue (Gerxhani, 2004). These issues necessitate changes and restrictions in the labour market. Skills training, language classes, and faster processes for recognizing foreign qualifications are all examples of reforms that may help refugees join the formal economy. Targeted aid for firms and sectors that may use more workers can also assist soften the blow to wages and employment levels.

Increasing labour market flexibility while safeguarding workers' rights should also be a priority for policymakers' actions. Incentives for firms that recruit refugees are one way to foster integration and more fairly divide the benefits of a larger labour pool while also supporting the local community. Regulations and changes of the labour market in the wake of a refugee influx, then, need to walk a fine line. They need to create conditions under which the labour market can absorb the influx of new workers without causing major hardship for the people who already make a living in the sector. These rules and changes are important not just for the host country's economy but also for social harmony and unity.

4.2 Policy Responses to Unemployment and Wage Pressures

Policy responses to unemployment and wage pressures, especially in the context of increased labour supply following a refugee inflow, require varied measures. While laying the framework for long-term economic integration and stability, these policies aim to relieve the current strain on the labour market. Governments frequently adopt active labour market policies (ALMPs) to deal with unemployment (Fossati, 2018). Job-seeker assistance, vocational education, and industry-specific financial incentives all fall under this category. These reforms are intended to help both locals and migrants become more marketable to potential employers, leading to a better job-seeker-employer match. Specifically, high-demand industries that can absorb more workers without major pay depression can be targeted through vocational training.

In a divided labour market with a sizable informal sector, wage pressures may be very severe. In this area of policy, efforts are typically made to fortify labour market institutions and enforcement mechanisms in order to better protect minimum wage requirements and worker rights. A race to the bottom in salaries and working conditions is often a problem when there is an oversupply of labour, but this can be avoided by bolstering these institutions. Furthermore, governments may launch public works programmes targeted at increasing employment possibilities, notably in infrastructure and service industries. Locals and migrants alike can benefit from these programmes because they create employment opportunities, which lowers the unemployment rate and increases the flow of money into the economy, which, in turn, boosts consumer spending and wages.

Reacting to unemployment and wage pressures can also be aided greatly by fiscal policy. Employment isn't the only upside to investing in public services and infrastructure; doing so also boosts economic output, which could eventually lead to greater salaries. Businesses that formally employ members of the local community and refugee populations might benefit from tax breaks and other forms of government aid (Lyon et al., 2007). Some nations have salary subsidy programmes to help workers out. Temporarily assisting businesses, these programmes ensure salaries remain at a level that prevents workers from losing purchasing power and ultimately their jobs. When the economy is in a slump or there has been an unexpected increase in the number of people looking for work, these types of subsidies can be quite helpful.

Last but not least, a concerted effort including government bodies, the corporate sector, and international organizations is required for effective policy responses to unemployment and wage pressures. It is extremely important for the international community to contribute financial aid and expertise to help implement effective labour market regulations in host nations dealing with high refugee populations. The goal of these regulations is to foster mutually beneficial economic integration that helps keep communities together even when times are tough.

4.3 *Effectiveness of Labour Market Regulations in Balancing the Needs of Local Citizens and Refugees*

There has been a lot of discussion on how to best calibrate labour market policies to meet the demands of both native-born workers and refugees. Regulations imposed on the labour market serve to safeguard employees, provide equitable compensation, and forestall abuse (Naidu et al., 2018). However, they can complicate efforts to meet the needs of both locals and refugees.

To begin, refugees may be unfairly affected by overly strict laws in the job market since they typically lack the social and economic capital of their host countries. For instance, if minimum salaries are mandated by law, businesses may favour hiring natives because of their superior command of the language and depth of experience in the field. On the other hand, looser rules may bring in a flood of low-wage workers, which could drive down wages, displace locals, and increase social tensions.

One way governments try to regulate the employment of migrants is by introducing work permits for refugees, with the goal of preventing unlawful work and exploitation (Taran, 2001). When done successfully, work permits can assist refugees acquire lawful employment and contribute to the economy without significantly disturbing the local labour market (Brell et al., 2020). For instance, it is in everyone's interest to take a sectoral strategy and issue work permits to refugees in fields that are now experiencing labour shortages. In addition, several nations have quota systems in place that restrict the number of refugees allowed to participate in specific industries (Castles & Ozkul, 2014). These caps are put in place to safeguard local salaries and job prospects from being undercut by an influx of foreign workers. However, it is difficult to find a middle ground between economic benefit and social acceptability when determining appropriate quotas.

To ensure that refugees and locals are treated equally in the labour market, legislation need to be backed up by enforcement mechanisms. This consists of labour law enforcement measures like routine inspections and sanctions for noncompliant firms. Unscrupulous firms may seek to hire undocumented refugees to avoid labour laws if restrictions aren't enforced properly, leading to a shadow economy that is bad for the state and its workers.

To maximize their economic contribution while minimizing rivalry with low-skilled local workers, refugees should be employed at appropriate skill levels, and regulations that promote the recognition of degrees and skills gained overseas can help with this. More swiftly and successfully integrating refugees into the workforce is another benefit of this method. The adaptability of labour market regulations is an important factor in determining their efficacy. Regulations need to be adaptive to changing economic situations and labour market dynamics. For example, during economic expansions, more lax rules could help fill labour shortages and stimulate economic activity, while during recessions, more restrictive measures might be necessary to protect local jobs.

5 Policy Effectiveness and Critique

5.1 *Critical Analysis of the Overall Effectiveness of Policies Implemented*

Economic consequences, social integration, and political stability are all relevant factors to consider when evaluating the success of programmes designed to mitigate the effect of refugee influxes on local labour markets. When evaluating the success of such policies critically, it is not uncommon to find an intricate web of intended results and unintended consequences. On one side, laws like work permits, labour quotas, and minimum wage enforcement are aimed to safeguard both refugees and host populations (Martin & Ruhs, 2019). They hope to stop vulnerable groups from being exploited and local labour markets from being undercut. However, these rules can have unforeseen results, such as making it harder for refugees to find work, expanding underground job markets, or encouraging companies to hire locally to avoid additional regulation.

In addition, the ability and willingness of government authorities to implement these policies is often crucial to their success. Even well-thought-out regulations can fail to achieve their goals if enforcement is inadequate or corruption is widespread. It's possible that this would cause the rules' intended protections for migrants and locals to be insufficient in practise.

When evaluating policies, it's important to think about how well they can adjust to new circumstances. For instance, protectionist labour policies might be tightly enforced during economic downturns to secure local employment, while more open policies might be required during labour shortages to fill gaps in the labour market (Auer et al., 2005). Therefore, the effectiveness of a policy may depend much on how rigidly or how flexibly it is implemented.

Another common criticism is that policies are too narrowly focused on the short-term effects on the labour market rather than the longer-term problems of social and economic integration. This may cause a rise in economically and socially divisive "siloed" policies that deal with labour market problems in the near term without planning for the future. Finally, the degree to which labour market policies contribute to or detract from the larger aim of social cohesion is another indicator of their efficacy. Those that are seen as fair and inclusive can foster understanding and unity between refugees and host communities, while those that are considered as unfair and exclusive can fuel tensions between the two.

5.2 *Discussion of Unintended Consequences and Policy-Driven Market Distortions*

Unforeseen problems and market distortions may result from emergency economic measures taken in reaction to disasters like an unexpected influx of refugees. These consequences might arise from policy initiatives that, while well-intentioned, may not completely account for the complexity and dynamism of economic systems.

Whenever policymakers take action, there may be unintended results that they didn't anticipate. For instance, the unintended consequence of protecting local jobs through stringent labour market rules could be a rise in the underground economy, where both refugees and some natives seek and find employment outside of the law. Due to underreporting, this change might reduce tax revenue, weaken protections for workers' rights, and impact the quality of statistics used to inform future policy decisions (Shelley, 2007). Similarly, pay limits meant to avoid the decline of local wages can occasionally lead to artificial labour shortages, as companies may find the fixed wage levels uneconomical, particularly in areas where refugees could fill low-skilled positions (Conard, 2016). Some sectors of the host country's economy may become less productive and less competitive as a result.

Changes in resource allocation and market outcomes as a direct result of policy interventions are referred to as policy-driven market distortions. If businesses are given tax breaks if they recruit a particular number of locals, for instance, they may start filling positions based on quotas rather than on productivity needs. Investments in industries that are not receiving government support could be crowded out by incentives for businesses that recruit migrants, further distorting the market.

Another component of market distortion occurs from direct assistance programmes. Such programmes, if not well managed, can slow the integration of refugees into the labour market and slow economic growth as a whole by creating dependency and reducing the incentive for both refugees and local inhabitants to seek jobs (Fasani et al., 2022). The influx of foreign aid linked to refugee help can also cause an appreciation of the local currency, which, in turn, reduces the competitiveness of exports and alters the trade balance (Lancaster, 2008). This phenomenon, which has various names like the "aid curse" and the "Dutch disease," can have lasting negative repercussions on the economic structure of the host country.

It is crucial for policymakers to foresee and lessen these distortions and unintended effects. This calls for thorough monitoring and evaluation methods to assess outcomes and implications, as well as cautious policy formulation and continual adjustment. Minimizing unintended consequences and ensuring that policy interventions lead to positive and lasting outcomes requires a comprehensive strategy that takes into account not only the immediate goals but also the broader economic backdrop.

5.3 Comparison with Other Countries' Policy Responses to Similar Crises

Insights into the spectrum of tactics and their relative efficacy can be gained by comparing the policy responses of different countries to similar situations, such as large-scale influxes of refugees. Different countries have different economic systems, institutional capacities, and political landscapes, all of which influence how they deal with similar difficulties in their own ways.

For instance, regional instability has also resulted in large numbers of refugees entering Turkey and Jordan. Turkey, a country with a sizable and diverse economy, has developed a set of measures that make it easier for refugees to enter the workforce and make a positive economic impact. By helping refugees find work, this strategy hoped to reduce the early burden on public services and infrastructure (Esen & Oğuş Binatlı, 2017). Despite difficulties, such measures have had mixed results in fostering economic resilience and broadening participation.

Jordan, on the other hand, has taken a more cautious approach, at first enforcing stringent work permit rules for refugees in order to safeguard the interests of its own residents in the labour market (Lenner & Turner, 2018). However, over time, these regulations have been altered to give more work permits and enhance the livelihoods of refugees. Since trade liberalization would benefit both countries, the international community backed these reforms (Lenner & Turner, 2019).

Another parallel can be drawn with Europe, specifically Germany, which saw a dramatic increase in asylum seekers and refugees that same year.

Germans were notably welcoming at first, and the country has since invested heavily in integration programmes like language and skills instruction to help refugees find work. This long-term strategy has been lauded for striking a good balance between humanitarian goals and economic realism, but it has also encountered political and societal obstacles (Heinemann, 2017).

Similarly, remarkable is Sweden's liberal treatment of refugee seekers and its extensive welfare system (Dahlstedt & Neergaard, 2019). However, this generosity has tested the country's ability to integrate migrants into its labour market and society, showing the difficulties of balancing immediate humanitarian help with lasting economic integration.

The success of policy solutions in all of these situations depends on the interaction between economic policies and other elements, including social services, political will, and public opinion. For instance, the amount of infrastructure and social cohesiveness already present can affect the results of stabilization economic measures like greater government investment in areas where refugees are concentrated.

The success of a country's policy response to a refugee crisis is often dependant on its capacity to adjust to changing conditions and learn from the experiences of others. The value of adaptability, the significance of consistent policymaking, and the advantages of working together across borders are all brought into sharp relief by international comparisons. They stress that effective solutions need to be tailored to specific national circumstances and evaluated continuously to meet growing difficulties and capitalize on new opportunities, rather than relying on a single, generic policy response.

6 Alternative Policy Strategies

6.1 Exploration of Potential Alternative Policies Not Yet Implemented

Exploration of prospective alternative policy solutions involves analysing choices that have not been enacted but offer promise for tackling economic and social challenges more effectively. Theoretical study, empirical information from other contexts, or a combination of creative thinking and lessons acquired from prior policy implementations are commonplace sources for these possibilities.

Increasing funding for initiatives to improve local communities is one possible policy approach. A more balanced regional development approach may reduce the risk of overburdening city infrastructure if resources were not concentrated only in urban areas where refugees are likely to reside. The incentive for people to move to cities would be diminished if investments were made in rural economies to increase employment prospects.

Special economic zones (SEZs) that allow for the co-employment of refugees and host-community members are an alternate approach that could be pursued. Foreign and domestic investment could be enticed into these zones thanks to tax breaks and less regulations. However, SEZs need to be properly crafted to minimize exploitation and maintain fair labour conditions in order to realize their full potential for creating jobs, fostering technology transfer, and promoting economic integration of refugees.

Public-private partnership (PPP) options for constructing infrastructure and delivering public services could also be investigated. Public resources are stretched thin because of the crisis, yet service delivery and infrastructure development might benefit from private sector investment and expertise. PPPs have the potential to be especially useful in the renewable energy, waste management, and housing markets, all of which are essential to sustainable development and can yield both short- and long-term financial gains (Cheng et al., 2021).

Using digital platforms to link the capabilities of refugees with the needs of the labour market could be an innovative approach to labour market policy. By allowing users to work remotely, these platforms have the potential to increase access to the labour market beyond a person's immediate geographical area. By taking use of the internet economy, local labour market pressures may be alleviated and refugees could find sustainable employment.

Finally, a shift towards policies that favour the growth of small and medium-sized firms (SMEs) could be essential. Small and medium-sized enterprises (SMEs) are held up as examples of what the economy needs to spur growth and employment (Ndiaye et al., 2018). Facilitating refugee-owned and local SMEs' access to capital, training, and markets has the potential to boost economic activity and create jobs without putting locals out of work.

Before being put into practise, various policy ideas must be thoroughly studied for their possible economic impact, social ramifications, and political viability. These policies can be fine-tuned through analysis, stakeholder input, and trial programmes to better meet the needs of both refugees and host communities. The development of alternative policies should also be dynamic, with the capacity to adjust based on input and changing conditions on the ground.

6.2 *Theoretical Basis and Expected Outcomes of These Alternative Policies*

Various economic principles and frameworks that foresee particular outcomes based on historical data, case studies, and predictive modelling provide the theoretical underpinning for various policy choices. For instance, the endogenous growth hypothesis underpins regional development programmes by arguing that spending money on things like education and research can generate long-term economic growth. Economic inequality is reduced, rural areas benefit from increased employment opportunities, and urban areas have less strain on their infrastructure as a result of a more evenly distributed population as a result of these policies.

Trade liberalization and the notion of comparative advantage inform the creation of special economic zones (SEZs), which are designed to help areas focus on producing the kind of goods and services for which they have a comparative advantage. The eventual goal is higher levels of economic growth, technological transfer, job creation, and foreign direct investment (Hazakis, 2014). This method, however, counts on legitimate government and safety nets to keep exploited workers at bay and promote growth for all.

Theories of fiscal federalism and the efficient supply of public goods support public-private partnerships (PPPs) because they argue for the use of private capital to fund, construct, and manage public services and infrastructure. The argument is that private companies with better management and a business incentive can provide services more effectively than government agencies (Keating & Keating, 2013). Results including faster infrastructure construction, better delivery of public services, and lower state fiscal burden are anticipated.

Digital labour market platforms are founded on the theory of frictional unemployment, which says that unemployment might occur because of the time it takes for workers to locate new jobs that fit their talents (Diamond, 2011). A shorter length of unemployment, more productive labour markets, and potentially more cross-border employment prospects are all outcomes that could result from the use of digital platforms to allow faster and more efficient job matching.

Finally, the Schumpeterian concept of "creative destruction," which says that economic progress is fuelled by innovation brought about by entrepreneurial initiatives, lends credence to the emphasis on SMEs (Autio et al., 2014). Refugees may be overrepresented in the informal economy, therefore policies that help small and medium-sized enterprises (SMEs) are likely to lead to economic diversification, innovation, and job creation in that sector and others like it.

Theoretical foundations like this give credence to the idea that new policies might improve the lives of refugees and help the economy of the countries that take them in to expand and create jobs. It is critical to conduct thorough pilot programmes and empirical research to ensure that these anticipated benefits are in line with realities on the ground and do not lead to unanticipated negative consequences.

6.3 *International Best Practices and Lessons Learned for Policy Formulation*

Policymakers have a wealth of information to draw on in the form of international best practises and lessons learnt from varied global experiences. These practises are guided by the achievements and failures of other countries in resolving economic crises, ensuring that future solutions are more resilient and effective.

Assessing the economic climate in its whole before enacting policy is a crucial best practise. Countries that have weathered economic storms in the past typically undergo a thorough diagnostic process. The structural adjustment programmes of the 1990s were contentious, but they did show how vital it is to first identify the root causes of a problem before proposing a solution (Reed, 2013). Countries who took the effort to adapt World Bank and IMF guidelines to their own circumstances fared better than those that blindly followed global best practises (Toussaint & Millet, 2010).

The value of involving relevant parties is another takeaway. Policy solutions that are effective are characterized by the participation of many levels of government, the private sector, civil society, and international organizations. Collaborative governance, as seen in the Scandinavian countries' approach to labour market reforms through negotiations and agreements between companies, unions, and the government, can lead to more sustainable and fair solutions (Ibsen et al., 2011).

Another emerging aspect is the need of openness and responsibility in the administration of policies. Trust and support for government efforts are more likely to flourish in nations where individuals are kept informed of policy developments and the results of those policies. The open way in which South Korea handled its economic crisis in the late 1990s is generally regarded as a factor in the country's quick recovery (Haggard & Mo, 2000). Another great practise is setting budgetary limits and bolstering them with targeted social safety nets. Maintaining fiscal discipline by balancing government spending and revenues can lead to long-term sustainability, as shown by countries like Canada and Australia, without jeopardizing social support supplied to the most disadvantaged communities (Eyraud et al., 2018).

Finally, one takeaway that leaps out is the importance of being able to adjust policies. The best policy solutions are flexible enough to adjust to new information and new conditions. Countries like Singapore, who were able to quickly adapt their policies to the changing circumstances of the global financial crisis of 2008, shown their resilience under pressure (Wilson, 2011). Incorporating these best practises and lessons into the policy formulation process can strengthen the resilience and responsiveness of economic strategy. It makes it possible for nations to devise and put into effect policies that can weather the turbulence of economic crises.

7 Policy Recommendations

Policies that foster long-term growth while simultaneously resolving short-term economic issues are essential for sustainable economic management. Green investments, which include financing renewable energy projects and assisting industries with a little environmental impact, are one policy that has been recommended. This not only helps the environment, but it also helps the economy by making more jobs available and stimulating more creativity. Private sector investment in sustainable practises can be encouraged by fiscal measures. Economic growth may be sustained if public funds are allocated more effectively, with a particular emphasis on high-impact areas like education, healthcare, and infrastructure. Investment in digital infrastructure to foster a digital economy can also be a game-changer for long-term fiscal planning.

Economic policymaking requires striking a compromise between immediate concerns and longer-term aspirations. Policymakers may need to prioritize stimulus measures in the short term to help the economy recover from recessions. Some examples include reduced or eliminated taxes, greater spending on social programmes, and short-term subsidies for important companies. But in the long run, it's crucial to switch to policies that guarantee budgetary sustainability, such as gradual fiscal reduction, pension system reform, and measures that widen the tax base. Long-term economic competitiveness depends on addressing skills mismatches, which can only be done through policies that promote continual education and training.

In situations where there are enormous societal issues, as the aftermath of a refugee crisis, it is especially important to integrate economic and humanitarian goals. Provision of inclusive financial services to marginalized populations is one policy option for achieving this integration, as it increases economic participation and decreases inequality. It is important that locals and refugees alike have access to vocational training as part of any policy that affects the labour market. Housing, healthcare, and education are all areas where public-private partnerships can be used to benefit residents and their communities. It is crucial that these measures foster social unity and economic autonomy rather of adding fuel to already-smouldering social fires.

8 Conclusion

This chapter has examined the economic difficulties Lebanon is experiencing as a result of the Syrian refugee crisis, as well as the various policy solutions to this issue and their consequences. The main results show that the Lebanese government and central bank have adjusted monetary and fiscal policies to lessen the immediate economic repercussions, albeit with varied outcomes. Implications for both the domestic labour force and the refugee population are substantial, yet the success of labour market laws and reforms has been highly variable.

The initiatives have been criticized for attempting to provide both short-term relief and the foundation for long-term economic stability. It is now abundantly clear that bold action at this economic juncture is required to guarantee that Lebanon will have a prosperous and equitable economic future. To address the entire scale of the crisis, the policies put in place so far were necessary but insufficient.

Economic policy in Lebanon must not just be reactive but also strategically forward-looking, incorporating lessons acquired from foreign best practises, as the country continues to negotiate this complex scenario. To promote prosperity and stability, Lebanon's economic policy trajectory going forward must be tightly aligned with humanitarian considerations. To ensure Lebanon emerges from this crisis with a stronger, more inclusive economy, this strategy will be crucial in not just resolving the current economic issues but also in constructing a resilient foundation that can survive future shocks and pressures.

References

Arnholtz, J., & Lillie, N. (2023). Posted work as an extreme case of hierarchised mobility. *Journal of Ethnic and Migration Studies*, 1–18.

Auer, P., Efendioğlu, Ü., & Leschke, J. (2005). *Active labour market policies around the world: Coping with the consequences of globalization*. International Labour Organization.

Autio, E., Kenney, M., Mustar, P., Siegel, D., & Wright, M. (2014). Entrepreneurial innovation: The importance of context. *Research policy, 43*(7), 1097–1108.

Ben Hassen, T. (2021). The state of the knowledge-based economy in the Arab world: Cases of Qatar and Lebanon. *EuroMed Journal of Business, 16*(2), 129–153.

Blinder, A. S., Ehrmann, M., Fratzscher, M., De Haan, J., & Jansen, D. J. (2008). Central bank communication and monetary policy: A survey of theory and evidence. *Journal of economic literature, 46*(4), 910–945.

Brell, C., Dustmann, C., & Preston, I. (2020). The labor market integration of refugee migrants in high-income countries. *Journal of Economic Perspectives, 34*(1), 94–121.

Cansunar, A. (2021). Who is high income, anyway? Social comparison, subjective group identification, and preferences over progressive taxation. *The Journal of Politics, 83*(4), 1292–1306.

Castles, S., & Ozkul, D. (2014). Circular migration: Triple win, or a new label for temporary migration? In *Global and Asian perspectives on international migration* (pp. 27–49). Springer International Publishing.

Chan, S. G., Ramly, Z., & Karim, M. Z. A. (2017). Government spending efficiency on economic growth: Roles of value-added tax. *Global Economic Review, 46*(2), 162–188.

Cheng, Z., Wang, H., Xiong, W., Zhu, D., & Cheng, L. (2021). Public–private partnership as a driver of sustainable development: Toward a conceptual framework of sustainability-oriented PPP. *Environment, Development and Sustainability, 23*, 1043–1063.

Conard, E. (2016). *The upside of inequality: How good intentions undermine the middle class*. Penguin.

Dahlstedt, M., & Neergaard, A. (2019). Crisis of solidarity? Changing welfare and migration regimes in Sweden. *Critical Sociology, 45*(1), 121–135.

David, A., Marouani, M. A., Nahas, C., & Nilsson, B. (2020). The economics of the Syrian refugee crisis in neighbouring countries: The case of Lebanon. *Economics of Transition and Institutional Change, 28*(1), 89–109.

De Groot, O. J., Bozzoli, C., Alamir, A., & Brück, T. (2022). The global economic burden of violent conflict. *Journal of Peace Research, 59*(2), 259–276.

Deng, T. (2013). Impacts of transport infrastructure on productivity and economic growth: Recent advances and research challenges. *Transport Reviews, 33*(6), 686–699.

Diamond, P. (2011). Unemployment, vacancies, wages. *American Economic Review, 101*(4), 1045–1072.

Esen, O., & Oğuş Binatlı, A. (2017). The impact of Syrian refugees on the Turkish economy: Regional labour market effects. *Social Sciences, 6*(4), 129.

Eyraud, L., Debrun, M. X., Hodge, A., Lledo, V. D., & Pattillo, M. C. A. (2018). *Second-generation fiscal rules: Balancing simplicity, flexibility, and enforceability.* International Monetary Fund.

Fakhoury, T., & Stel, N. (2023). EU engagement with contested refugee returns in Lebanon: The aftermath of resilience. *Geopolitics, 28*(3), 1007–1032.

Fasani, F., Frattini, T., & Minale, L. (2022). (The Struggle for) Refugee integration into the labour market: Evidence from Europe. *Journal of Economic Geography, 22*(2), 351–393.

Fossati, F. (2018). Who wants demanding active labour market policies? Public attitudes towards policies that put pressure on the unemployed. *Journal of Social Policy, 47*(1), 77–97.

Furman, J., & Summers, L. H. (2019). Who's afraid of budget deficits? *Foreign Affairs, 98*(2), 82–95.

Gerxhani, K. (2004). The informal sector in developed and less developed countries: A literature survey. *Public choice, 120*(3-4), 267–300.

Ha, J., Kose, M. A., & Ohnsorge, F. (Eds.). (2019). *Inflation in emerging and developing economies: Evolution, drivers, and policies.* World Bank Publications.

Haffert, L., & Mehrtens, P. (2015). From austerity to expansion? Consolidation, budget surpluses, and the decline of fiscal capacity. *Politics & Society, 43*(1), 119–148.

Haggard, S., & Mo, J. (2000). The political economy of the Korean financial crisis. *Review of International Political Economy, 7*(2), 197–218.

Harting, P. (2021). Macroeconomic stabilization and long-term growth: The role of policy design. *Macroeconomic Dynamics, 25*(4), 924–969.

Hazakis, K. J. (2014). The rationale of special economic zones (SEZs): An I nstitutional approach. *Regional Science Policy & Practice, 6*(1), 85–101.

Heinemann, A. M. (2017). The making of 'good citizens': German courses for migrants and refugees. *Studies in the Education of Adults, 49*(2), 177–195.

Herbst, A. F., Wu, J. S., & Ho, C. P. (2014). Quantitative easing in an open economy—Not a liquidity but a reserve trap. *Global Finance Journal, 25*(1), 1–16.
Herwartz, H., & Theilen, B. (2021). Government ideology and fiscal consolidation: Where and when do government parties adjust public spending? *Public Choice, 187*(3–4), 375–401.
Iacoviello, M. (2005). House prices, borrowing constraints, and monetary policy in the business cycle. *American economic review, 95*(3), 739–764.
Ibsen, C. L., Larsen, T. P., Madsen, J. S., & Due, J. (2011). Challenging Scandinavian employment relations: The effects of new public management reforms. *The International Journal of Human Resource Management, 22*(11), 2295–2310.
Imam, P. A., & Jacobs, D. (2014). Effect of corruption on tax revenues in the Middle East. *Review of Middle East Economics and Finance, 10*(1), 1–24.
Jacobsen, K. (2002). Livelihoods in conflict: The pursuit of livelihoods by refugees and the impact on the human security of host communities. *International migration, 40*(5), 95–123.
Janmyr, M. (2022). Refugee participation through representative committees: UNHCR and the Sudanese committee in Beirut. *Journal of Refugee Studies, 35*(3), 1292–1310.
Kancs, D. A., & Lecca, P. (2018). Long-term social, economic and fiscal effects of immigration into the EU: The role of the integration policy. *The World Economy, 41*(10), 2599–2630.
Kaplan, S. B. (2016). Banking unconditionally: The political economy of Chinese finance in Latin America. *Review of International Political Economy, 23*(4), 643–676.
Keating, B., & Keating, M. (2013). Private firms, public entities, and microeconomic incentives: Public private partnerships (PPPs) in Australia and the USA. *International Journal of Organizational Analysis, 21*(2), 176–197.
Kelley, N. (2017). Responding to a refugee influx: Lessons from Lebanon. *Journal on Migration and Human Security, 5*(1), 82–104.
Kharroubi, S., Naja, F., Diab-El-Harake, M., & Jomaa, L. (2021). Food insecurity pre-and post the COVID-19 pandemic and economic crisis in Lebanon: Prevalence and projections. *Nutrients, 13*(9), 2976.
Klein, B., & Staal, K. (2017). Was the American recovery and reinvestment act an economic stimulus? *International Advances in Economic Research, 23*(4), 395–404.
Klein, M. C., & Pettis, M. (2020). *Trade wars are class wars: How rising inequality distorts the global economy and threatens international peace.* Yale University Press.
Lancaster, C. (2008). *Foreign aid: Diplomacy, development, domestic politics.* University of Chicago Press.
Lenner, K., & Turner, L. (2018). Learning from the Jordan compact. *Forced Migration Review, 57*, 48–51.

Lenner, K., & Turner, L. (2019). Making refugees work? The politics of integrating Syrian refugees into the labor market in Jordan. *Middle East Critique, 28*(1), 65–95.

Lyon, F., Sepulveda, L., & Syrett, S. (2007). Enterprising refugees: Contributions and challenges in deprived urban areas. *Local Economy, 22*(4), 362–375.

Martin, P., & Ruhs, M. (2019). Labour market realism and the global compacts on migration and refugees. *International Migration, 57*(6), 80–90.

Naidu, S., Posner, E. A., & Weyl, G. (2018). Antitrust remedies for labor market power. *Harvard law review, 132*(2), 536–601.

Ndiaye, N., Razak, L. A., Nagayev, R., & Ng, A. (2018). Demystifying small and medium enterprises'(SMEs) performance in emerging and developing economies. *Borsa Istanbul Review, 18*(4), 269–281.

Nseir, A. (2022). *Determinants of house prices in Lebanon: An ARDL approach.* Doctoral dissertation, Notre Dame University-Louaize.

Ray, S., Jain, S., Thakur, V., & Miglani, S. (2023). Evolution of the Finance Tracks Agendas. In *Global Cooperation and G20: Role of Finance Track* (pp. 85–176). Singapore.

Reed, D. (2013). *Structural adjustment, the environment and sustainable development.* Routledge.

Rostagno, M., Altavilla, C., Carboni, G., Lemke, W., Motto, R., Saint Guilhem, A., & Yiangou, J. (2021). *Monetary policy in times of crisis: A tale of two decades of the European Central Bank.* Oxford University Press.

Shelley, T. (2007). *Exploited: Migrant labour in the new global economy.* Zed Books.

Stiglitz, J. E. (2015). Macroeconomic fluctuations, inequality, and human development. In *Macroeconomics and Human Development* (pp. 31–58). Routledge.

Taran, P. A. (2001). Human rights of migrants: Challenges of the new decade. *International Migration, 38*(6), 7–51.

Tooze, A. (2018). *Crashed: How a decade of financial crises changed the world.* Penguin.

Toussaint, E., & Millet, D. (2010). *Debt, the IMF, and the World Bank: Sixty questions, sixty answers.* NYU Press.

Traum, N., & Yang, S. C. S. (2015). When does government debt crowd out investment? *Journal of Applied Econometrics, 30*(1), 24–45.

Turner, L. (2015). Explaining the (non-) encampment of Syrian refugees: Security, class and the labour market in Lebanon and Jordan. *Mediterranean politics, 20*(3), 386–404.

Wilson, P. (2011). *Challenges for the Singapore economy after the global financial crisis.* World Scientific.

Yen, S. H., Ong, W. L., & Ooi, K. P. (2015). Income and employment multiplier effects of the Malaysian higher education sector. *Margin: The Journal of Applied Economic Research, 9*(1), 61–91.

CHAPTER 8

Navigating the International Response: Aid, Diplomacy, and Economic Support in Lebanon's Refugee Crisis

1 Introduction

The Syrian refugee crisis, precipitated by a decade-long conflict, has unfolded into one of the most significant humanitarian emergencies of our time, with repercussions felt across the globe. Lebanon, a small country with its own complex socio-political landscape, has found itself at the epicentre of this crisis, hosting millions of Syrian refugees. This influx has strained Lebanon's already fragile infrastructure, economy, and social fabric, presenting an unprecedented challenge that demands a robust international response. This chapter provides a critical examination of the international community's efforts to address these challenges through aid, diplomatic initiatives, and economic support mechanisms.

The significance of the international response to Lebanon cannot be overstated. As a frontline state in the Syrian refugee crisis, Lebanon's stability and capacity to provide for refugees and its own population are of paramount concern not only for regional stability but also for the broader international community. The chapter outlines the multifaceted nature of international aid, which encompasses humanitarian assistance, financial support, and investments in infrastructure and public services. This support aims to alleviate the immediate needs of refugees and host communities, while also bolstering Lebanon's economic resilience and infrastructure to ensure long-term sustainability.

M. Zreik, *The Syrian Refugee Crisis and Lebanon's Economic Landscape*, https://doi.org/10.1007/978-3-031-68471-5_8

However, the response has been met with a myriad of challenges. Coordination between Lebanese authorities, international organizations, and donor countries has been fraught with difficulties, leading to inefficiencies and gaps in aid delivery and support mechanisms (Lehmann & Masterson, 2020). Moreover, the chapter highlights the impact of diplomatic relations on the efficacy of economic support, illustrating how geopolitical considerations can influence the flow of aid and investment into the country.

Despite these challenges, the international community's engagement in Lebanon represents a critical lifeline for millions of individuals affected by the Syrian crisis. This chapter sets the stage for a deeper analysis of the effectiveness of these efforts, the obstacles encountered, and the lessons learned. By providing an overview of the international response's significance for Lebanon, it lays the groundwork for subsequent sections that will delve into the specifics of aid delivery, diplomatic initiatives, and the broader implications for international cooperation in crisis contexts. Through this comprehensive examination, this chapter aims to contribute to a nuanced understanding of the global cooperation required to navigate the complexities of the Syrian refugee crisis in Lebanon.

2 Framework of International Aid

2.1 *Types of Aid Provided*

In the face of the Syrian refugee crisis, Lebanon has received a multifaceted array of international aid, aimed at mitigating the impacts of the influx on both the refugee population and the host community. This aid can be broadly categorized into humanitarian, financial, and infrastructural support, each addressing different facets of the crisis and its repercussions on Lebanon's socio-economic fabric.

Humanitarian aid, the most immediate form of assistance, has been pivotal in providing lifesaving support to refugees and vulnerable populations within Lebanon. This includes food assistance, shelter, medical care, and education services (Buckner et al., 2018). The international community, through various UN agencies and non-governmental organizations (NGOs), has mobilized resources to ensure that basic human needs are met, aiming to alleviate the suffering caused by displacement and the ongoing conflict in Syria. The distribution of this aid, however, has been challenged by the sheer scale of the crisis and the need for effective coordination among a multitude of actors.

Financial support, on the other hand, has been directed towards both immediate relief efforts and long-term economic stabilization. Grants and loans from international financial institutions and bilateral donors have sought to strengthen Lebanon's economic resilience in the face of the added strain from the refugee population (Hamadeh, 2022). This financial assistance has been critical in supporting the Lebanese government's capacity to maintain public services and infrastructure, which are essential for both refugees and the host community. It has also included targeted support for small and medium-sized enterprises (SMEs) and cash assistance programmes designed to stimulate the local economy and provide vulnerable families with the means to sustain themselves (Hamdar et al., 2017).

Infrastructural support constitutes a significant portion of the international aid directed towards Lebanon, recognizing that the country's existing infrastructure was under considerable stress even before the refugee crisis. Investments have been made in critical sectors such as water, sanitation, healthcare, and education (Sumpf et al., 2016). The aim is to not only address the immediate needs exacerbated by the refugee influx but also to contribute to the long-term development and resilience of Lebanon's infrastructure. This includes projects designed to expand access to clean water, improve sanitation facilities in refugee-hosting areas, enhance the capacity of healthcare facilities to cater to increased demand, and rehabilitate schools to accommodate the surge in student numbers (Wardeh & Marques, 2023).

The framework of international aid to Lebanon, encompassing humanitarian, financial, and infrastructural support, reflects a comprehensive approach to addressing both the immediate and enduring challenges posed by the Syrian refugee crisis. While this support has been indispensable in managing the impacts of the crisis, the delivery and effectiveness of aid are subject to ongoing assessment and adaptation to meet the evolving needs of both refugees and the host community in Lebanon.

2.2 *Distribution and Management*

The distribution and management of international aid in Lebanon, in response to the Syrian refugee crisis, involve a complex network of actors, each playing a crucial role in ensuring that the assistance reaches those in need effectively and efficiently. This system of aid delivery has been characterized by its reliance on international organizations, non-governmental organizations (NGOs), and the Lebanese government, each contributing unique strengths and facing distinct challenges in the process.

International organizations, particularly those under the United Nations umbrella, have been instrumental in orchestrating the global response to the refugee crisis in Lebanon. They bring to the table a wealth of experience in managing humanitarian operations, the ability to mobilize substantial resources, and a mandate that allows for coordination across borders and among various stakeholders (Geha & Talhouk, 2019). These organizations operate through well-established mechanisms for aid distribution, which include direct assistance programmes, funding local NGOs, and partnering with government agencies. However, their efforts are often hampered by the bureaucratic complexities inherent in large international bodies, leading to delays in aid delivery and challenges in adapting to the rapidly changing ground realities (Thorvaldsdottir et al., 2021).

NGOs, both local and international, play a pivotal role in the distribution and management of aid on the ground. Their agility, local knowledge, and direct access to affected communities allow for a more nuanced and responsive approach to aid delivery. NGOs often act as the implementing partners for international organizations, translating strategic objectives into tangible assistance for individuals and communities. Yet, their effectiveness can be limited by resource constraints, competition for funding, and, at times, overlapping efforts that can lead to inefficiencies and duplication of services.

The Lebanese government's role in managing the international aid response is complex, given the country's limited resources and the political sensitivities surrounding the refugee issue (Nassar & Stel, 2019). The government is responsible for coordinating with international donors and organizations, setting policy frameworks, and ensuring that aid aligns with national priorities and regulations (Najem, 2016). This coordination is facilitated through various mechanisms, including the Lebanon Crisis Response Plan, which aims to bridge the humanitarian-development divide (Carpi & Pınar Şenoğuz, 2019). Despite these efforts, the government faces significant challenges in managing the scale of the crisis, including infrastructural strains, social tensions, and the overarching need for systemic reforms to enhance governance and accountability.

The interplay between these actors in the distribution and management of international aid in Lebanon highlights a multifaceted system striving to address an unprecedented crisis. While the collaboration has yielded significant achievements in providing relief and support to refugees and host communities, the experience also underscores the importance of enhancing coordination, streamlining processes, and fostering partnerships that can adapt to the evolving dynamics of the crisis.

3 Diplomatic Initiatives and Economic Support

3.1 Diplomatic Efforts

The diplomatic initiatives undertaken to support Lebanon in the wake of the Syrian refugee crisis have been a cornerstone of the international response, aiming to marshal global support and resources to address both the immediate needs and long-term challenges faced by the country. These efforts have been characterized by a multi-pronged approach, involving high-level negotiations, international conferences, and bilateral agreements, each designed to facilitate a cohesive and effective international stance towards the crisis.

High-level diplomatic engagements have been pivotal in raising awareness and securing commitments from the international community. Summits and conferences hosted by the United Nations, the European Union, and other international entities have served as critical platforms for discussing the impacts of the refugee crisis on Lebanon and the broader region (Ignatieff et al., 2016). These gatherings have been instrumental in mobilizing financial aid, with donor countries pledging support to meet the humanitarian needs of refugees and the infrastructural demands of host communities. Moreover, they have facilitated dialogue on the importance of shared responsibility, emphasizing the need for a global approach to address the displacement crisis.

Bilateral diplomatic efforts have also been significant, with Lebanon engaging directly with individual countries to secure both political support and financial assistance. These bilateral interactions have enabled Lebanon to negotiate terms of aid that are aligned with its national priorities, including support for public services, infrastructure development, and economic stabilization measures. Through these direct negotiations, Lebanon has been able to secure critical funding and investments, underscoring the importance of diplomatic relations in the context of international assistance.

Furthermore, diplomatic initiatives have extended beyond traditional state actors to include engagements with international financial institutions and private sector stakeholders (Chedrawi et al., 2020). These interactions have been crucial in facilitating economic support measures, including loans and grants aimed at bolstering Lebanon's economy. The involvement of these entities has highlighted the multifaceted nature of diplomatic efforts, where economic and financial strategies are integrated into the broader framework of international support.

The impact of these diplomatic efforts on garnering international support for Lebanon cannot be overstated. Through a combination of high-level summits, bilateral negotiations, and engagements with financial institutions, Lebanon has been able to secure a lifeline of support that addresses both the immediate humanitarian needs and the long-term economic challenges posed by the refugee crisis. These diplomatic initiatives have underscored the critical role of international solidarity and cooperation in responding to global crises, demonstrating the potential for collective action to mitigate the impacts of displacement on host countries like Lebanon.

3.2 Economic Support Measures

Economic support measures for Lebanon in response to the Syrian refugee crisis have been multifaceted, encompassing a broad spectrum of financial assistance and economic stabilization programmes. These initiatives, spearheaded by international financial institutions and donor countries, have been crucial in addressing the immediate and long-term economic challenges faced by Lebanon, exacerbated by the massive influx of refugees. The design and implementation of these programmes reflect a strategic approach aimed at bolstering Lebanon's economic resilience while providing direct support to both the refugee population and host communities.

Financial assistance has been provided in various forms, including grants, loans, and direct budget support (Araji et al., 2019). Grants from international donors have targeted specific sectors such as education, healthcare, and infrastructure, aiming to alleviate the immediate pressures on Lebanon's public services. Loans, particularly from international financial institutions like the World Bank and the International Monetary Fund, have offered longer-term economic support, focusing on structural reforms and economic stabilization efforts (Dakhlallah, 2020). These loans are often accompanied by technical assistance to ensure effective implementation and to support Lebanon's capacity to manage and utilize the funds efficiently.

Economic stabilization programmes have played a critical role in mitigating the impact of the refugee crisis on Lebanon's economy. These programmes have included initiatives aimed at supporting small and medium-sized enterprises (SMEs), enhancing job creation, and fostering economic growth. For instance, some programmes have focused on the development of the private sector as a means to absorb the economic shock of the refugee influx by promoting entrepreneurship and providing vocational training to both Lebanese citizens and Syrian refugees (Verme et al., 2015). This approach not only aims to stimulate economic activity but also to integrate refugees into the labour market, reducing their dependency on humanitarian aid.

Moreover, international support has extended to direct cash assistance programmes for vulnerable populations, both Lebanese and refugees. These programmes are designed to inject liquidity into the local economy while providing immediate relief to those most in need (Chaaban et al., 2020). By ensuring that families have the means to purchase goods and services, these cash assistance programmes support local businesses and contribute to the stability of the local economy.

The economic support measures for Lebanon, provided by international financial institutions and donor countries, represent a comprehensive effort to address the multifaceted challenges posed by the Syrian refugee crisis. Through a combination of financial assistance, economic stabilization programmes, and direct support to individuals, these initiatives aim to strengthen Lebanon's economic foundation, promote sustainable growth, and ensure that both the host community and refugees can navigate the challenges of displacement with resilience and dignity.

3.3 *Impact on Lebanon's Economy*

The diplomatic and economic efforts undertaken to support Lebanon in the face of the Syrian refugee crisis have had a significant impact on the country's economic resilience. These efforts, encompassing a wide array of financial assistance and stabilization programmes, have aimed to mitigate the immediate challenges while laying the groundwork for long-term economic recovery. Assessing the effectiveness of these initiatives reveals a complex picture, with tangible benefits as well as areas requiring further attention to fully realize their potential in bolstering Lebanon's economy.

On the positive side, the influx of international aid has provided crucial support to Lebanon's public finances, directly relieving the government's budgetary pressures. Financial assistance, including grants and concessional loans, has enabled the Lebanese government to maintain essential services such as education, healthcare, and infrastructure, which were under severe strain due to the increased demand from both the refugee and host populations (Joseph et al., 2021). This support has been instrumental in preventing a complete collapse of public services, thereby maintaining a semblance of economic stability and social cohesion.

Economic stabilization programmes have also contributed to economic resilience by focusing on structural reforms and supporting sectors critical to Lebanon's economic growth. Initiatives aimed at enhancing the private sector, promoting job creation, and improving infrastructure have had positive effects on economic activity (Ben Hassen, 2021). By supporting small and medium-sized enterprises and fostering an environment conducive to business, these programmes have helped to stimulate economic growth and reduce unemployment rates, albeit to varying degrees of success (Chaaban et al., 2018).

However, the effectiveness of these diplomatic and economic efforts has been tempered by several challenges. Despite the significant amount of aid and support received, Lebanon continues to grapple with profound economic difficulties, including high levels of public debt, currency devaluation, and inflation (Dakhlallah, 2020). The scale of the refugee crisis, combined with pre-existing economic vulnerabilities, has placed an immense burden on the country's economy, making it difficult for international support alone to reverse the tide of economic decline. Additionally, issues related to aid distribution, coordination among donors, and the efficient use of funds have at times hindered the full impact of the support provided.

Moreover, the sustainability of economic support measures is a concern. While immediate relief and stabilization efforts are critical, there is a pressing need for initiatives that address the underlying structural issues of Lebanon's economy. This includes reforms in governance, public sector efficiency, and fiscal policy, which are essential for long-term economic resilience but have been challenging to implement due to political complexities (Traboulsi, 2019).

4 Challenges in International Cooperation

4.1 Coordination Challenges

The coordination of aid and support among international actors, non-governmental organizations (NGOs), and the Lebanese government in response to the Syrian refugee crisis has presented significant challenges, complicating efforts to deliver effective assistance. These difficulties stem from a variety of factors, including the diversity of stakeholders involved, varying priorities and approaches, and the complex political and social landscape of Lebanon.

One of the primary challenges in coordinating international cooperation is the sheer number of actors involved, each with their own mandates, operational strategies, and funding mechanisms. International organizations, bilateral donors, multilateral agencies, and a myriad of NGOs have converged on Lebanon to offer support (Makhoul et al., 2023). While the intention is to cover a broad spectrum of needs, from immediate humanitarian relief to long-term economic stabilization, the multiplicity of actors often leads to overlaps in aid distribution, gaps in coverage, and sometimes even competition for visibility and resources (El Chaarani & Raimi, 2022). This can result in inefficiencies and a dilution of efforts, where resources are not optimally allocated to where they are most needed.

Moreover, the varying priorities and approaches of different donors and implementing agencies can hinder effective coordination. For instance, while some actors may prioritize immediate humanitarian assistance, others might focus on infrastructure development or economic reform initiatives. Reconciling these different priorities requires robust coordination mechanisms and a shared understanding of the multifaceted nature of the crisis, which is often difficult to achieve. Additionally, the alignment of international support with the Lebanese government's priorities and capacities is crucial but challenging, given the country's complex political environment and governance issues.

The Lebanese government's capacity to coordinate and manage the influx of international aid and support efforts is another significant challenge. Limited resources, political divisions, and bureaucratic hurdles can impede effective collaboration and integration of international assistance within national response plans (Fakhoury, 2021). The government's ability to act as an effective conduit for channelling aid and ensuring it reaches the intended beneficiaries is critical for the success of these efforts.

However, political sensitivities, particularly concerning the long-term presence of refugees and their integration into Lebanese society, further complicate coordination efforts.

Effective communication and information sharing among all stakeholders are vital for overcoming these coordination challenges. However, establishing and maintaining open lines of communication is often difficult in practice. The lack of a centralized platform for tracking aid flows, sharing best practices, and coordinating interventions across the myriad of actors can lead to redundancies and missed opportunities for synergies.

Despite these challenges, efforts have been made to improve coordination, such as the establishment of the Lebanon Crisis Response Plan (LCRP), which aims to bring together the various stakeholders under a unified strategic framework (Carpi & Pınar Şenoğuz, 2019). While such mechanisms represent steps in the right direction, ongoing challenges underscore the need for enhanced collaboration, flexibility, and a commitment to a shared vision for addressing the complex needs arising from the Syrian refugee crisis in Lebanon. Overcoming these coordination hurdles is essential for ensuring that aid is delivered efficiently, effectively, and in a manner that addresses both immediate needs and the longer-term resilience of refugees and host communities alike.

4.2 Efficacy and Limitations of Aid

The efficacy of international aid and economic support in response to crises, such as the Syrian refugee situation in Lebanon, is a subject of considerable debate, reflecting a complex interplay of achievements and limitations. While aid has undeniably provided critical support to both refugees and host communities, its effectiveness is often curtailed by various limitations and unintended consequences that can undermine the goals of these interventions.

A primary limitation of international aid is its often-short-term focus, aimed at addressing immediate humanitarian needs without sufficiently tackling the underlying causes or ensuring sustainable development. This approach can lead to a dependency syndrome, where recipient communities become reliant on external assistance for survival, without fostering self-sufficiency or resilience. In Lebanon, the continuous need for humanitarian aid to support the Syrian refugee population has highlighted the challenge of transitioning from emergency aid to long-term development solutions that empower the affected communities.

Moreover, the effectiveness of aid is frequently hampered by coordination issues among the myriad of actors involved, including international organizations, NGOs, and the Lebanese government (Nassar & Stel, 2019). These coordination challenges can lead to duplication of efforts, gaps in service provision, and inefficiencies in resource allocation. The complexity of navigating the political and operational landscape in Lebanon further complicates the delivery of aid, sometimes diverting resources away from the most critical needs due to bureaucratic hurdles or political considerations.

Another significant limitation is the alignment of aid with the actual needs of the target populations. Misalignments can occur due to inadequate needs assessments, lack of community involvement in planning and implementing aid programmes, or the prioritization of donor interests over recipient needs. Such misalignments can lead to interventions that are either ineffective or, in some cases, counterproductive, exacerbating vulnerabilities or social tensions between refugees and host communities.

Unintended consequences of international aid and economic support can also manifest in various ways, potentially undermining the stability and economic health of the host country. For instance, large influxes of aid can have inflationary effects, distort local markets, or create labour market imbalances (Stiglitz, 2015). In Lebanon, the presence of a large refugee population, coupled with significant amounts of humanitarian aid, has raised concerns about labour market distortions and competition for jobs, contributing to tensions between the refugees and the Lebanese host communities.

Furthermore, aid can inadvertently contribute to governance issues by relieving the host government of its responsibilities to provide public services and uphold the rights of all individuals within its territory. This can weaken the social contract between the state and its citizens, with long-term implications for governance and stability.

5 Case Studies: Successes and Shortcomings

5.1 Successful Initiatives

The landscape of international aid and support in response to the Syrian refugee crisis in Lebanon is marked by numerous initiatives, each with its own set of outcomes and lessons learned. Among these, certain case studies stand out for their success, providing valuable insights into what makes aid efforts effective and impactful. These successful initiatives highlight the importance of tailored approaches, community involvement, and strong coordination among stakeholders.

One such example is the education-focused programmes that have been instrumental in addressing the educational needs of Syrian refugee children in Lebanon. Organizations like UNICEF, in partnership with the Lebanese Ministry of Education and Higher Education, have implemented the "Reaching All Children with Education" (RACE) strategy (Jalbout, 2015). This initiative has been successful in integrating refugee children into the Lebanese public education system, providing formal and non-formal education opportunities. The success of RACE can be attributed to its comprehensive approach, which includes capacity building for teachers, rehabilitation of school infrastructure, and provision of learning materials (Al-Hroub et al., 2023). The programme's emphasis on inclusivity and resilience-building among students, coupled with its alignment with national educational policies, has ensured its effectiveness and sustainability.

Another successful initiative involves the support for small and medium-sized enterprises (SMEs) aimed at boosting economic resilience among Lebanese host communities and Syrian refugees. Programmes funded by international donors and implemented by NGOs and local partners have provided financial grants, technical training, and market access to SMEs. These efforts have not only contributed to economic growth but also facilitated social cohesion by promoting entrepreneurship across communities (Hamdar et al., 2017). The success of these programmes lies in their participatory design, which considers the specific needs and potentials of local economies, and their focus on creating sustainable livelihood opportunities.

The water and sanitation sector also provides a noteworthy case study, where international aid has significantly improved access to clean water and sanitation facilities for both refugees and host communities. Projects have included the construction and rehabilitation of water infrastructure, such as pipelines and treatment plants, and hygiene promotion activities (Gharios & Farajalla, 2020). The success of these interventions is largely due to effective collaboration between international NGOs, local authorities, and the communities themselves. By ensuring that projects are community-led and context-specific, these efforts have not only improved health outcomes but also enhanced community ownership and sustainability of the infrastructure.

These successful case studies share common factors contributing to their effectiveness: a strong emphasis on collaboration and coordination among various stakeholders, including government bodies, international organizations, and the communities served; the adaptability and responsiveness of programmes to the changing needs of the target populations; and a focus on sustainability and capacity building within local systems. Moreover, these initiatives have demonstrated the value of integrating aid efforts into national strategies and frameworks, ensuring that they complement and reinforce the host country's own development goals.

5.2 *Shortcomings and Lessons Learned*

In the realm of international aid and support, particularly within the context of Lebanon's response to the Syrian refugee crisis, not all endeavours have met their intended objectives. The analysis of less successful initiatives offers critical insights into the complexities of aid delivery and the importance of adaptability, coordination, and local engagement. These shortcomings provide valuable lessons for improving future international responses to similar crises.

One notable area of challenge has been in the sector of housing and shelter for refugees. Despite significant efforts and resources directed towards providing adequate shelter for Syrian refugees, many initiatives have struggled due to a combination of regulatory constraints, limited scalability, and logistical challenges. In some cases, projects aimed at constructing or improving refugee housing encountered regulatory barriers that delayed or restricted implementation (Rozo & Sviatschi, 2021). These experiences underscore the importance of engaging with local authorities and stakeholders early in the planning process to ensure that projects are feasible within the existing regulatory and social landscape.

Another area where shortcomings have been observed is in the employment and livelihood programmes aimed at integrating refugees into the local economy. While these programmes are crucial for reducing dependency on aid and promoting self-reliance among refugee populations, some have fallen short due to a lack of alignment with local market needs and the skills of the refugee population. Additionally, the competition for jobs between refugees and host community members has sometimes exacerbated tensions, highlighting the need for careful planning and community engagement to ensure that livelihood programmes contribute positively to social cohesion and economic stability (Hynie, 2018).

The effectiveness of aid distribution itself has also faced challenges, particularly in terms of ensuring equity and transparency in the allocation of resources. In some instances, aid has been distributed unevenly, with certain groups receiving more support than others due to logistical challenges or gaps in data and assessment methodologies (Meininghaus, 2016). This has led to perceptions of unfairness and, in some cases, increased tension between different communities. These experiences highlight the critical need for robust needs assessment processes, transparent decision-making, and continuous monitoring and evaluation to ensure that aid reaches those most in need.

From these shortcomings, several key lessons have emerged for future international responses. First, the importance of flexibility and adaptability in programme design and implementation cannot be overstated. Crises are dynamic, and interventions must be able to adjust to changing conditions and needs. Second, the engagement of local communities and authorities from the outset is essential for ensuring the feasibility, acceptance, and sustainability of aid efforts. Building local capacity and fostering ownership among local stakeholders can enhance the effectiveness and longevity of interventions.

Furthermore, coordination among the myriad of actors involved in crisis response efforts is crucial for minimizing duplication of efforts, filling gaps in service provision, and maximizing the impact of limited resources. Establishing clear mechanisms for coordination and communication can help align efforts and leverage the strengths of different actors.

Lastly, the importance of comprehensive needs assessments and data-driven approaches to aid delivery has been underscored. Understanding the specific needs, capacities, and dynamics of affected populations and host communities is essential for designing interventions that are both effective and equitable.

These lessons learned from less successful endeavours highlight the complexities of delivering international aid in crisis contexts. They stress the need for a nuanced, collaborative, and adaptive approach to humanitarian assistance, one that recognizes the diverse and evolving needs of affected populations and the contexts in which they live.

6 Recommendations for Enhanced International Support

6.1 Optimizing Aid Delivery

Enhancing the efficiency and effectiveness of international aid delivery, especially in complex crisis situations like the Syrian refugee crisis in Lebanon, requires a multifaceted approach that addresses the challenges and lessons learned from past endeavours. Central to optimizing aid delivery is the need for improved coordination, community involvement, and the adoption of data-driven strategies.

A critical recommendation for improving aid delivery is the enhancement of coordination mechanisms among all stakeholders involved in the aid process. This includes establishing more robust platforms for communication and information sharing among international organizations, NGOs, donor agencies, and the Lebanese government. Such platforms can facilitate the mapping of ongoing initiatives, identification of gaps and overlaps, and the development of a more unified and strategic approach to aid distribution. Furthermore, joint planning and response mechanisms can help ensure that aid delivery is aligned with the priorities of both the affected populations and the host country's development goals.

Incorporating community involvement in the planning, execution, and monitoring of aid programmes is another essential strategy for optimizing aid delivery. Engaging with communities not only ensures that aid initiatives are responsive to the actual needs and preferences of those they aim to assist but also fosters a sense of ownership and empowerment among beneficiaries. This involvement can take various forms, from community consultations to participatory planning processes and feedback mechanisms that allow for the continuous adaptation of programmes based on community input.

Adopting a data-driven approach to aid delivery is also crucial for enhancing its efficiency and effectiveness. This involves the systematic collection, analysis, and use of data to inform decision-making processes. By leveraging data on needs assessments, programme outcomes, and resource allocation, aid organizations can more accurately target interventions, measure their impact, and adjust strategies as necessary. Additionally, data transparency and sharing among stakeholders can improve accountability and trust in the aid process, ensuring that resources are used effectively and reach those most in need.

Finally, investing in local capacity building is essential for sustainable aid delivery. Supporting the development of local institutions, NGOs, and community groups can enhance local resilience and reduce dependency on external aid over time. This includes providing training, resources, and technical assistance to strengthen the ability of local actors to manage and implement aid programmes, ensuring that the knowledge and skills remain within the community long after international actors have departed.

By implementing these recommendations, international support for crises like the Syrian refugee crisis in Lebanon can be made more efficient, effective, and responsive to the needs of all stakeholders involved. Optimizing aid delivery in this manner not only addresses immediate humanitarian needs but also contributes to the longer-term resilience and development of affected communities.

6.2 *Strengthening Diplomatic and Economic Partnerships*

Strengthening diplomatic and economic partnerships is essential for supporting Lebanon's long-term economic stability and infrastructure development, particularly in the context of the challenges posed by the Syrian refugee crisis. To enhance international cooperation and partnerships, a strategic, multifaceted approach is necessary, focusing on building resilient frameworks that can withstand the complexities of current and future crises.

One key recommendation is to foster deeper, more strategic diplomatic engagements between Lebanon and its international partners. This involves not only increasing the quantity of interactions but also enhancing the quality of these engagements to ensure they are focused on mutual interests and long-term goals. High-level dialogues and bilateral talks should be regularized, creating a continuous platform for exchange and cooperation. These engagements can serve as a foundation for developing comprehensive support strategies that address both immediate humanitarian needs and the structural reforms required for economic stability and growth.

Enhancing economic partnerships is equally critical. International donors, financial institutions, and Lebanon's trading partners should work together to create investment frameworks that encourage sustainable economic growth. This could include mechanisms such as investment guarantees, risk-sharing facilities, and incentives for private sector investment in key sectors like renewable energy, water management, and digital infrastructure. Such initiatives not only bolster Lebanon's economy but also create jobs and improve services for both Lebanese citizens and Syrian refugees, contributing to social stability and cohesion.

Additionally, leveraging international financial institutions' expertise and resources to support Lebanon's economic reform agenda is vital. These institutions can provide not only financial assistance but also technical advice on implementing reforms that enhance governance, improve public financial management, and stimulate economic growth. By aligning international support with Lebanon's reform priorities, partners can ensure that aid and investments have a lasting impact, strengthening the country's resilience to economic shocks and crises.

Collaboration on regional initiatives that address common challenges such as climate change, water scarcity, and regional trade can also strengthen diplomatic and economic partnerships. Regional cooperation can facilitate shared solutions that benefit Lebanon and its neighbours, promoting stability and prosperity across the region. Such initiatives require coordinated diplomatic efforts and the establishment of regional forums for dialogue and cooperation.

7 Conclusion

The comprehensive examination of international aid, diplomatic initiatives, and economic support in response to the Syrian refugee crisis in Lebanon has highlighted both the multifaceted nature of the international community's efforts and the complex challenges these endeavours face. Through the critical analysis of aid delivery mechanisms, the exploration of diplomatic efforts to garner support, the assessment of economic support measures, and the reflection on both successes and shortcomings, this chapter has underscored the indispensable role of international cooperation in addressing the profound impacts of the crisis on Lebanon.

The insights gained from the detailed case studies of successful initiatives have illuminated the pathways through which international support can effectively meet the immediate needs of refugees and host communities while laying the groundwork for long-term resilience and development. Conversely, the examination of less successful endeavours has provided valuable lessons on the importance of adaptability, local engagement, and the need for a holistic approach to crisis management.

Recommendations for optimizing aid delivery and strengthening diplomatic and economic partnerships have pointed towards a future direction that emphasizes enhanced coordination, community involvement, data-driven strategies, and investment in local capacity. These strategies are not only crucial for improving the effectiveness of current efforts but are also essential for preparing Lebanon and the international community to address similar challenges in the future.

References

Al-Hroub, A., Tilawi, A., & Jouni, N. (2023). Equitable and inclusive education in Lebanon: Policies and practices for special needs learners in Lebanon. In *School inclusion in Lebanon: Integrating research on students with giftedness and learning disabilities into practice* (pp. 1–24). Springer International Publishing.

Araji, S., Hlasny, V., Mansour Ichrakieh, L., & Intini, V. (2019). Targeting debt in Lebanon: A structural macro-econometric model. *Middle East Development Journal, 11*(1), 75–104.

Ben Hassen, T. (2021). The state of the knowledge-based economy in the Arab world: Cases of Qatar and Lebanon. *EuroMed Journal of Business, 16*(2), 129–153.

Buckner, E., Spencer, D., & Cha, J. (2018). Between policy and practice: The education of Syrian refugees in Lebanon. *Journal of Refugee Studies, 31*(4), 444–465.

Carpi, E., & Pınar Şenoğuz, H. (2019). Refugee hospitality in Lebanon and Turkey. On making 'the Other'. *International Migration, 57*(2), 126–142.

Chaaban, J., Chalak, A., Ismail, T., & Taha, H. (2018). *Assessing EU–Mediterranean policies in the field of industry from a bottom-up perspective: The case of lebanon* (No. 27). MEDRESET working papers.

Chaaban, J., Salti, N., Ghattas, H., Moussa, W., Irani, A., Jamaluddine, Z., & Al-Mokdad, R. (2020). *Multi-purpose cash assistance in Lebanon: Impact evaluation on the well-being of Syrian refugees.* American University of Beirut Press. https://www.aub.edu.lb/fafs/agri/aedrg/Documents/AUB%20Impact%20Study_Final_print.pdf

Chedrawi, C., Osta, A., & Osta, S. (2020). CSR in the Lebanese banking sector: A neo-institutional approach to stakeholders' legitimacy. *Journal of Asia Business Studies, 14*(2), 143–157.

Dakhlallah, K. M. (2020). Public debt and fiscal sustainability: The cyclically adjusted balance in the case of Lebanon. *Middle East Development Journal, 12*(2), 340–359.

El Chaarani, H., & Raimi, L. (2022). Determinant factors of successful social entrepreneurship in the emerging circular economy of Lebanon: Exploring the moderating role of NGOs. *Journal of Entrepreneurship in Emerging Economies, 14*(5), 874–901.

Fakhoury, T. (2021). Power-sharing after the Arab Spring? Insights from Lebanon's political transition. In *Power-sharing after civil war* (pp. 9–26). Routledge.

Geha, C., & Talhouk, J. (2019). From recipients of aid to shapers of policies: Conceptualizing government–United Nations relations during the Syrian refugee crisis in Lebanon. *Journal of Refugee Studies, 32*(4), 645–663.

Gharios, G., & Farajalla, N. (2020). Connecting various investments plans to address new challenges in the current water management structure of Lebanon. *Water Utility Journal, 24*, 49–61.

Hamadeh, H. (2022). *Lebanon's financial crisis and the international monetary fund*. Doctoral dissertation, Lebanese American University.

Hamdar, B. C., Najjar, R., & Karameh, K. (2017). The Lebanese perception of the impact of small & medium enterprises (SMEs) on the national economy. *Journal of Economics and Public Finance, 3*(3), 330–342.

Hynie, M. (2018). Refugee integration: Research and policy. *Peace and Conflict: Journal of Peace Psychology, 24*(3), 265.

Ignatieff, M., Keeley, J., Ribble, B., & McCammon, K. (2016). *The refugee and migration crisis: Proposals for action, UN Summit 2016*. Brookings Institution.

Jalbout, M. (2015). *Reaching all children with education in Lebanon*. Brookings: World.

Joseph, J., Katsos, J. E., & Daher, M. (2021). Local business, local peace? Intergroup and economic dynamics. *Journal of Business Ethics, 173*, 835–854.

Lehmann, M. C., & Masterson, D. T. (2020). Does aid reduce anti-refugee violence? evidence from Syrian refugees in Lebanon. *American Political Science Review, 114*(4), 1335–1342.

Makhoul, J., El Ashkar, C., Mialon, M., Levy, A., Sabbagh, D., & Nakkash, R. (2023). Benefits and risks: Views of humanitarian organizations in Lebanon on corporate assistance. *PLOS Global Public Health, 3*(11), e0002291.

Meininghaus, E. (2016). Humanitarianism in intra-state conflict: Aid inequality and local governance in government-and opposition-controlled areas in the Syrian war. *Third World Quarterly, 37*(8), 1454–1482.

Najem, Y. E. (2016). *International donors and urban planning policy and practice: The European Union in Lebanon*. Doctoral dissertation.

Nassar, J., & Stel, N. (2019). Lebanon's response to the Syrian refugee crisis–Institutional ambiguity as a governance strategy. *Political Geography, 70*, 44–54.

Rozo, S. V., & Sviatschi, M. (2021). Is a refugee crisis a housing crisis? Only if housing supply is unresponsive. *Journal of Development Economics, 148*, 102563.

Stiglitz, J. E. (2015). Macroeconomic fluctuations, inequality, and human development. In *Macroeconomics and Human Development* (pp. 31–58). Routledge.

Sumpf, D., Isaila, V., & Najjar, K. (2016). *The impact of the Syria crisis on Lebanon* (pp. 269–308). Springer International Publishing.

Thorvaldsdottir, S., Patz, R., & Eckhard, S. (2021). International bureaucracy and the United Nations system: Introduction. *International Review of Administrative Sciences, 87*(4), 695–700.

Traboulsi, R. I. (2019). *Risk mitigation practices of the Lebanese banking sector: A proactive approach to maintain resilience through prudential regulations.* Nottingham Trent University.

Verme, P., Gigliarano, C., Wieser, C., Hedlund, K., Petzoldt, M., & Santacroce, M. (2015). *The welfare of Syrian refugees: Evidence from Jordan and Lebanon.* World Bank Publications.

Wardeh, M., & Marques, R. C. (2023). Measuring the SDGs in refugee camps: An insight into Arab States Bordering Syria. *Sustainability, 15*(2), 1720.

CHAPTER 9

Forward Momentum: Future Projections and Strategic Recommendations for Lebanon Amidst the Refugee Crisis

1 Introduction

In the face of the Syrian refugee crisis, Lebanon finds itself at a critical juncture, grappling with multifaceted challenges that threaten its economic stability, social fabric, and long-term development. This chapter embarks on a forward-looking journey, aiming to chart a course for Lebanon's future amidst these unprecedented challenges. This chapter is not merely an academic exercise; it is a clarion call for action, offering a blueprint for resilience, recovery, and sustainable growth in a nation that has found itself host to an extraordinary number of refugees relative to its size.

The chapter sets out to provide a nuanced understanding of the economic and social trajectories Lebanon may encounter in the coming years. It delves into the complexities of the refugee crisis, not only as a humanitarian emergency but also as a pivotal factor influencing Lebanon's development path. By synthesizing insights from the preceding analyses, this chapter offers a holistic view of the potential futures facing Lebanon. It critically examines the current trends, challenges, and external factors that will shape the nation's economic and social landscape.

The penultimate chapter synthesizes insights from previous analyses to project future economic and social trajectories for Lebanon. It proposes a set of strategic recommendations aimed at fostering resilience and sustainable development. Furthermore, this chapter acknowledges the dual

M. Zreik, *The Syrian Refugee Crisis and Lebanon's Economic Landscape*, https://doi.org/10.1007/978-3-031-68471-5_9

imperative facing Lebanon: addressing immediate humanitarian needs while laying the groundwork for long-term economic planning and social integration. It recognizes that the Syrian refugee crisis, while posing significant challenges, also presents opportunities for Lebanon to strengthen its resilience and embark on a path of sustainable development.

To navigate this complex terrain, the chapter proposes a comprehensive set of strategic recommendations tailored for both the Lebanese government and the international community. These recommendations are grounded in a deep understanding of the multifaceted impacts of the crisis on Lebanon's economy, labour market, inflation, trade dynamics, and the broader regional context. They are designed to foster economic stability, promote social cohesion, and ensure that Lebanon can emerge from this crisis stronger and more united.

In advocating for these strategic interventions, the chapter emphasizes the importance of collaborative efforts and multilateral approaches. It highlights the role of public-private partnerships (PPPs), community-based initiatives, and international cooperation in addressing the challenges and seizing the opportunities presented by the refugee crisis. Through a concerted and coordinated response, Lebanon can chart a course towards recovery and growth, ensuring a prosperous future for all its residents, both Lebanese and refugees.

2 Economic and Social Trajectories

2.1 Future Economic Projections

The Syrian refugee crisis has left an indelible mark on Lebanon, a country already beset by economic vulnerabilities and political instability. As Lebanon navigates through these tumultuous times, understanding the future economic projections becomes crucial for crafting effective policies and strategies. The economic ramifications of the refugee crisis are multifaceted, influencing various sectors and dimensions of Lebanon's economy. This analysis endeavours to shed light on potential future economic scenarios for Lebanon, taking into account the current trends and the array of external factors at play.

The influx of refugees has exerted considerable pressure on Lebanon's public services, infrastructure, and labour markets, exacerbating existing economic challenges. However, it's essential to recognize that the crisis also presents opportunities for economic transformation and development if strategically managed. Lebanon's economy, characterized by its resilience in the face of adversity, is at a crossroads, with the potential for divergent future trajectories.

One potential scenario envisages a Lebanon that successfully leverages international support and investments to not only address the immediate needs stemming from the refugee crisis but also to lay the foundation for sustainable economic growth. In this scenario, targeted investments in infrastructure, education, and healthcare, coupled with reforms aimed at improving the business environment, could spur economic activity and create job opportunities for both Lebanese citizens and Syrian refugees. Such developments could lead to increased social cohesion and a more robust, diversified economy less susceptible to external shocks.

Conversely, there exists a more sombre scenario where Lebanon struggles to cope with the continued strain of the refugee presence, compounded by limited international support and internal political deadlock. In this scenario, public services remain overstretched, unemployment rates soar, and economic growth stagnates. The absence of comprehensive policy responses and international cooperation could lead to increased social tensions and further economic decline, pushing Lebanon into a prolonged period of instability and hardship.

The determining factors between these scenarios lie in the policy choices made by Lebanese policymakers and the extent of international support and collaboration. The crisis requires a balanced approach that considers the immediate humanitarian needs while also focusing on long-term economic resilience and development. Lebanon's future economic trajectory will significantly depend on its ability to implement reforms, attract investments, and foster an inclusive economy that benefits all residents—Lebanese and refugees alike.

Moreover, the regional and global economic environment will play a pivotal role in shaping Lebanon's economic future. Factors such as global economic trends, oil prices, and regional stability can influence Lebanon's economic performance and its ability to recover and grow in the aftermath of the crisis (Baumann, 2021). The international community's response to the refugee crisis, including aid effectiveness, investment, and trade policies, will also have profound implications for Lebanon's economic landscape.

2.2 *Social Implications*

The presence of Syrian refugees in Lebanon has not only economic but profound social implications, weaving a complex tapestry of challenges and opportunities that will shape the nation's social fabric for years to come. Lebanon's experience with the refugee crisis is emblematic of the broader social dynamics at play in countries hosting large refugee populations, where the immediate humanitarian response gradually transitions into long-term social integration and cohesion issues (Nourpanah & Poteet, 2016).

One of the most pressing social challenges is the strain on Lebanon's public services, including education, healthcare, and housing, which has been exacerbated by the refugee influx. This situation has heightened tensions between host communities and refugees, as competition for limited resources can lead to friction and social unrest (Anouti & Enna, 2023). The increased demand has also exposed and magnified existing inadequacies within Lebanon's public service infrastructure, challenging the country to address these systemic issues while ensuring equitable access for all residents (Abi Ghanem, 2018).

Moreover, the refugee presence has implications for Lebanon's demographic landscape and social cohesion. The integration of a large number of refugees into Lebanese society poses both a challenge and an opportunity to foster a more inclusive and cohesive community. It necessitates policies and initiatives that promote mutual understanding, respect, and cooperation between refugees and host communities. Successfully navigating this integration can strengthen Lebanon's social fabric, but failure to do so may exacerbate divisions and hinder social stability.

However, amidst these challenges lie significant opportunities for Lebanon to enhance its social resilience and cohesion. The crisis has catalysed a broad-based response from Lebanese civil society, international NGOs, and community-based organizations, fostering a spirit of solidarity and cooperation (Sukkari, 2023). This collaborative approach not only addresses immediate needs but also builds stronger community bonds and enhances social capital, which are crucial for Lebanon's long-term social development.

Furthermore, the refugee presence offers an opportunity for cultural exchange and enrichment, as Syrians and Lebanese share many cultural and historical ties. The interaction between these communities can lead to a greater appreciation of cultural diversity, fostering a more inclusive society that values and leverages its multicultural identity.

3 Policy Recommendations for the Lebanese Government

3.1 Economic Stability and Growth

In the face of the Syrian refugee crisis, the Lebanese government faces the dual challenge of managing immediate humanitarian needs while ensuring long-term economic stability and growth. Achieving this balance requires a nuanced approach to policymaking, with a focus on sustainable fiscal policies, strategic investment in infrastructure, and targeted sectoral development. These recommendations are not merely prescriptive measures but a roadmap towards a resilient and thriving Lebanese economy, capable of weathering current challenges and seizing future opportunities.

Fiscal policy plays a pivotal role in Lebanon's quest for economic stability. It is imperative for the government to implement comprehensive fiscal reforms aimed at reducing public debt levels while ensuring sufficient funding for critical social services. This involves improving tax collection mechanisms, broadening the tax base to include untapped sectors, and combating tax evasion. Fiscal discipline, coupled with transparent and accountable public spending, can restore confidence among investors and international financial institutions, opening the door to increased financial support and investment.

Investment in infrastructure is another cornerstone of economic recovery and growth. Lebanon's public infrastructure, strained by years of underinvestment and further burdened by the refugee influx, requires urgent and substantial upgrades. Focusing on sectors such as transportation, energy, water, and telecommunications can not only improve the quality of life for all residents but also enhance the country's attractiveness to investors. Public-private partnerships can be a viable model for infrastructure development, leveraging private sector expertise and resources for public good. Moreover, infrastructure projects can create job opportunities, stimulating economic activity and providing employment for both Lebanese citizens and Syrian refugees, thereby easing social tensions.

Sectoral development is equally critical for Lebanon's economic revival. Prioritizing sectors that have a comparative advantage or high growth potential, such as information technology, agriculture, and tourism, can drive economic diversification and resilience. Supporting these sectors through targeted policies, such as incentives for innovation, investment in research and development, and improvements in market access, can catalyse growth. Additionally, focusing on the development of small and medium-sized enterprises (SMEs), which constitute the backbone of Lebanon's economy, can foster entrepreneurship and create jobs (Hamdar et al., 2017). Sector-specific strategies should also include measures for integrating refugees into the labour market, ensuring that economic growth is inclusive and benefits all segments of society.

3.2 *Labour Market and Employment*

The Syrian refugee crisis has significantly impacted Lebanon's labour market, introducing both challenges and opportunities. The influx of refugees has increased labour supply, particularly in informal sectors, which has, in some cases, led to lower wages and increased competition for jobs (Kikano et al., 2021). However, this situation also presents an opportunity to revitalize and expand the labour market, ensuring it is inclusive, diverse, and capable of supporting economic growth and social integration.

A strategic approach to labour market reform and job creation in Lebanon must start with the formalization of the informal sector. This involves creating a regulatory framework that encourages businesses to enter the formal economy, thereby increasing government revenue through taxes and improving workers' access to social protections. Formalization should be complemented by initiatives designed to enhance skill development among both Lebanese citizens and Syrian refugees. Vocational training programmes, tailored to meet the needs of key growth sectors, can equip individuals with the skills necessary for employment in areas where there is a demand for labour. Such programmes not only improve employability but also foster economic diversification.

Moreover, Lebanon can adopt policies that stimulate job creation by supporting entrepreneurship and small and medium-sized enterprises (SMEs), which are crucial drivers of economic growth and employment. Providing access to finance, simplifying business registration processes, and offering tax incentives are measures that can encourage business formation and expansion. Additionally, public-private partnerships can be leveraged to invest in large-scale infrastructure projects and public services, creating jobs and improving the overall business environment.

Integrating refugees into the economy is another critical aspect of Lebanon's labour market strategy. This requires a balanced approach that considers the rights and needs of refugees as well as the concerns of host communities. Policies aimed at integration should include work permit reforms to ease access to formal employment for refugees, coupled with measures that protect Lebanese workers from unfair competition. Furthermore, integrating refugees into the labour market can be facilitated through targeted training programmes that align refugees' skills with the needs of the local economy, thus turning the refugee population into an asset rather than a burden.

3.3 Social Cohesion and Integration

In the context of Lebanon's multifaceted challenges exacerbated by the Syrian refugee crisis, fostering social cohesion and integration becomes paramount. The country's social fabric is under immense strain, necessitating deliberate and thoughtful policies that encourage unity, mutual respect, and a sense of shared community between Lebanese citizens and Syrian refugees (Akar, 2016). Achieving social cohesion in such a complex environment requires a comprehensive approach that goes beyond mere coexistence to actively promote integration and equitable access to services for all residents.

To cultivate a sense of belonging and community among refugees and host populations, it is essential to implement policies that facilitate interactions and mutual understanding. Initiatives such as community centres and joint educational programmes can serve as platforms for cultural exchange and dialogue, helping to dispel myths, build trust, and foster a sense of shared identity. These spaces can also provide access to essential services, including education, healthcare, and legal assistance, ensuring that refugees and vulnerable Lebanese populations receive the support they need.

Equitable access to services is crucial for social cohesion and requires targeted interventions to address existing disparities. The Lebanese government, with support from international organizations and NGOs, must work to strengthen public service infrastructure, particularly in education, healthcare, and housing. Ensuring that all residents have access to quality services not only addresses immediate needs but also builds a foundation for long-term stability and integration. Policies should focus on expanding capacity and improving the quality of services, with special attention to areas most affected by the refugee influx.

Moreover, promoting economic inclusion is a vital component of social cohesion. Economic policies that create job opportunities for both Lebanese citizens and Syrian refugees can reduce competition and tensions over resources. Initiatives that support small and medium-sized enterprises, provide vocational training, and facilitate access to the labour market for refugees are essential. By improving economic prospects for all, these policies can contribute to a sense of shared progress and prosperity.

Finally, communication and community engagement are key to successful integration and social cohesion. Transparent and inclusive dialogue about the challenges and benefits of refugee integration can help manage expectations and mitigate tensions. Engaging community leaders and local organizations in the planning and implementation of policies ensures that interventions are contextually relevant and culturally sensitive, enhancing their effectiveness and sustainability.

4 Strategies for International Support

4.1 Enhancing Aid Effectiveness

The Syrian refugee crisis has underscored the necessity for robust international support mechanisms to aid host countries like Lebanon, which bear the brunt of regional upheavals. The effectiveness of international aid, however, hinges on its delivery and coordination with Lebanese authorities, ensuring that assistance is not only timely but also aligns with the nation's immediate needs and long-term development goals. Optimizing international aid delivery entails a multifaceted approach, focusing on enhancing coordination, ensuring transparency, and adapting aid to the evolving context of Lebanon's socio-economic landscape.

Central to enhancing aid effectiveness is the need for strengthened coordination between international donors, Lebanese authorities, and non-governmental organizations (NGOs). A coordinated approach ensures that aid efforts are not duplicated and resources are channelled where they are most needed. Establishing a centralized platform for information sharing and decision-making can facilitate this coordination, allowing for real-time updates on the ground realities and aid requirements. Such a platform can serve as a nexus for aligning the strategies of various stakeholders, ensuring that international support complements Lebanon's national priorities and the specific needs of both Lebanese citizens and Syrian refugees.

Transparency in the allocation and utilization of aid funds is another crucial element in optimizing aid effectiveness. Transparent mechanisms for tracking aid flows increase accountability, build trust among stakeholders, and ensure that funds reach their intended beneficiaries (Linders, 2013). Implementing standardized reporting and auditing processes, accessible to all stakeholders, can enhance transparency. This not only helps in evaluating the impact of aid interventions but also in identifying areas where adjustments are needed to improve outcomes.

Adapting international aid to the evolving context in Lebanon is essential for addressing both immediate humanitarian needs and supporting long-term development. As Lebanon navigates through economic challenges and social tensions exacerbated by the refugee crisis, international aid strategies must be flexible and responsive to changing circumstances. This includes shifting from short-term emergency assistance to long-term development support, focusing on economic recovery, infrastructure development, and social cohesion initiatives. Tailoring aid to support policy reforms, capacity building, and resilience efforts can provide Lebanon with the foundation needed to manage current challenges and prepare for a sustainable future.

4.2 Supporting Economic Recovery

International partners play a crucial role in supporting Lebanon's path to economic recovery amidst the challenges posed by the Syrian refugee crisis and compounded by existing economic vulnerabilities. The collaboration between Lebanon and its international allies can take various forms, each aimed at revitalizing the Lebanese economy through strategic interventions such as trade facilitation, investment, and debt relief. These measures are not just acts of goodwill; they are investments in regional stability and global prosperity, recognizing that Lebanon's economic health has far-reaching implications.

Trade facilitation stands out as a pivotal strategy for economic recovery, offering a pathway for Lebanon to boost its exports and integrate more deeply into global markets. International partners can assist by simplifying customs procedures, reducing trade barriers, and supporting Lebanon in meeting international trade standards. This assistance can significantly enhance Lebanon's export competitiveness, opening up new markets for

Lebanese products and services. Furthermore, trade facilitation can attract foreign direct investment (FDI) by signalling a conducive business environment, essential for economic revitalization (Othman, 2022).

Investment in key sectors of the Lebanese economy is another critical area where international partners can contribute to Lebanon's economic recovery. Sectors such as renewable energy, technology, infrastructure, and tourism hold significant potential for growth and job creation. International partners can support these sectors through direct investments, partnerships with Lebanese businesses, and financing of development projects. Such investments not only spur economic activity but also help diversify Lebanon's economy, making it more resilient to external shocks. Encouraging public-private partnerships, especially in infrastructure projects, can further leverage international expertise and capital for Lebanon's benefit.

Debt relief is an essential consideration in the context of Lebanon's economic recovery. The country's high public debt burden limits its fiscal space and undermines economic stability (Badra, 2022). International partners, including bilateral and multilateral lenders, can offer debt relief or restructuring solutions to alleviate this burden. By easing the debt load, Lebanon can redirect resources towards critical areas such as social services, infrastructure development, and economic reforms. Debt relief measures can also improve Lebanon's creditworthiness, attracting further investment and support from the international community.

4.3 *Fostering Regional Stability*

The Syrian refugee crisis, with Lebanon at its epicentre, extends beyond national borders, touching on broader regional stability and international peace. Addressing its implications necessitates concerted diplomatic and regional initiatives that go beyond immediate humanitarian responses to encompass long-term strategies for peace and stability. Fostering regional stability in the wake of such a crisis requires a multifaceted approach that combines diplomatic efforts, regional cooperation, and support for inclusive governance and development.

Diplomatic efforts aimed at resolving the underlying conflicts that fuel the refugee crisis are paramount. International actors, including governments, intergovernmental organizations, and non-state actors, must work together to facilitate dialogue and negotiations among conflicting parties in Syria. The goal of these diplomatic efforts should be to achieve a sustainable peace that addresses the root causes of displacement, allowing refugees to voluntarily return home in safety and dignity. Engaging in constructive diplomacy requires patience, commitment, and a willingness to address the complex political, ethnic, and religious dynamics that underpin the conflict (Blakemore, 2019).

Beyond diplomacy, regional cooperation is essential to manage the refugee crisis and its impact on stability effectively. Neighbouring countries, along with regional organizations, should collaborate to share the burden of hosting refugees, coordinate humanitarian assistance, and develop joint strategies for economic resilience and social integration. This cooperation can mitigate the strain on individual host countries like Lebanon and prevent the crisis from exacerbating existing regional tensions. Moreover, regional initiatives can foster a sense of shared responsibility and solidarity, essential components for building a stable and peaceful Middle East.

Support for inclusive governance and sustainable development within refugee-hosting countries is another critical aspect of fostering regional stability. International partners should assist countries like Lebanon in strengthening their governance structures, ensuring that all communities, including refugees, are represented and have access to services. Promoting inclusive governance helps to address grievances that could lead to social unrest, while investment in sustainable development ensures that countries can provide for their citizens and refugees alike, reducing the likelihood of economic collapse or conflict.

5 Collaborative Efforts and Multilateral Approaches

5.1 *Public-Private Partnerships*

The dynamic and complex challenges posed by the Syrian refugee crisis in Lebanon call for innovative and sustainable solutions, particularly in the realms of economic development and service delivery. Public-private partnerships (PPPs) emerge as a vital tool in this context, bridging the gap between the public sector's regulatory and strategic capabilities and the efficiency, expertise, and resources of the private sector (Villani et al., 2017). These collaborative arrangements can play a transformative role in addressing the needs of both Lebanese citizens and Syrian refugees, fostering economic resilience and ensuring the provision of essential services.

PPPs offer a mechanism for leveraging private sector investment in public projects, which is particularly crucial in times of fiscal constraint and economic uncertainty. By involving private entities in the financing, design, construction, and operation of infrastructure and services, PPPs can enhance quality and efficiency, reduce costs, and accelerate project delivery. This is especially relevant for Lebanon, where public infrastructure has been overwhelmed by the demands of a growing population, including a significant number of refugees. Through PPPs, Lebanon can improve its transportation networks, energy supply, water and sanitation services, and telecommunications infrastructure, which are all critical for economic development and the well-being of its population.

Furthermore, public-private partnerships can drive innovation and technology transfer, contributing to more sustainable and resilient economic growth (Pandey et al., 2022). The private sector's propensity for innovation can introduce new technologies and practices in public services and infrastructure projects, leading to better outcomes and more effective responses to the challenges posed by the refugee crisis. This is particularly important in sectors like renewable energy, waste management, and digital services, where innovative solutions can significantly impact Lebanon's sustainability and economic prospects.

In addition to economic benefits, PPPs can also enhance social cohesion and integration by ensuring that infrastructure projects and service delivery are designed to meet the needs of all community members, including the most vulnerable. By involving a range of stakeholders in the planning and implementation phases, PPPs can ensure that projects are inclusive and address the specific challenges faced by refugee populations, such as access to education, healthcare, and employment opportunities.

However, the success of PPPs in Lebanon requires a supportive legal and regulatory framework, clear and transparent procurement processes, and mechanisms for effective partnership management and risk sharing. Building the capacity of public institutions to engage with private partners, negotiate contracts, and oversee projects is also crucial for maximizing the benefits of PPPs.

5.2 Community-Based Initiatives

The fabric of Lebanese society, intricately woven with threads of diverse communities, faces unprecedented strain due to the Syrian refugee crisis. Amidst this backdrop, community-based initiatives emerge as beacons of hope and resilience, underscoring the power of grassroots efforts in driving sustainable development and fostering social integration. These initiatives, rooted in the unique needs and capacities of local communities, offer a participatory approach to addressing the challenges posed by the crisis, ensuring that solutions are both relevant and sustainable.

Community-based initiatives empower local populations by involving them directly in the development process, from planning to implementation and evaluation. This bottom-up approach ensures that projects are closely aligned with the community's specific needs, increasing their effectiveness and sustainability. In Lebanon, where the impact of the refugee crisis varies significantly across different regions, such localized strategies are particularly crucial. They can address a wide range of issues, from improving access to education and healthcare to creating economic opportunities and enhancing public infrastructure, all the while promoting social cohesion and mutual understanding between Lebanese citizens and Syrian refugees.

Moreover, supporting community-based initiatives fosters a sense of ownership and agency among local populations, crucial for building resilience in the face of adversity. When communities are actively engaged in identifying problems and devising solutions, they are more likely to be invested in the success of these initiatives, leading to more sustainable and impactful outcomes. This participatory approach also helps to bridge divides, build trust, and strengthen the social fabric, laying the groundwork for long-term peace and stability.

Community-based initiatives also serve as a platform for innovation, allowing for the testing and scaling of novel approaches to development challenges (Archer et al., 2014). By drawing on local knowledge and resources, these initiatives can develop creative and context-specific solutions that larger, top-down programmes may overlook. This flexibility and adaptability are particularly valuable in a rapidly changing environment like Lebanon's, where the needs of communities can evolve quickly due to economic, social, or political shifts.

However, the potential of community-based initiatives can only be fully realized with adequate support from both the Lebanese government and international partners. This includes providing financial resources, capacity building, and policy frameworks that enable community-led development. Encouraging partnerships between community organizations, NGOs, the private sector, and government agencies can further amplify the impact of these initiatives, creating synergies and leveraging diverse resources and expertise.

5.3 International Cooperation

In the shadow of the Syrian refugee crisis, the imperative for strengthened international cooperation and multilateral efforts cannot be overstated (Dimitrova et al., 2018). The crisis transcends national borders, affecting regional stability and posing significant humanitarian, economic, and social challenges. Lebanon, at the forefront of this crisis, bears a disproportionate burden, underscoring the need for a collaborative global response. International cooperation is critical not only in addressing the immediate needs of refugees and host communities but also in tackling the root causes of displacement and facilitating durable solutions.

The complexity of the refugee crisis demands a coordinated approach that leverages the strengths and resources of a broad spectrum of actors, including nations, international organizations, non-governmental organizations (NGOs), the private sector, and civil society. This multilateral engagement is essential for marshalling the necessary financial support, technical expertise, and humanitarian assistance. Moreover, international cooperation fosters the sharing of best practices and innovations, enhancing the effectiveness and efficiency of response efforts.

A key aspect of strengthening international cooperation involves addressing the root causes of the crisis, notably the ongoing conflict in Syria. Diplomatic efforts aimed at achieving a political solution are crucial and require the concerted effort of the international community. By working together to promote peace and stability in Syria, the international community can contribute to reducing the number of people forced to flee, ultimately addressing one of the fundamental drivers of the crisis.

In addition to addressing the causes of displacement, international cooperation is vital in supporting host countries like Lebanon. This support should not be limited to humanitarian aid but should also include development assistance that addresses long-term economic and social impacts. International partners can play a significant role in supporting infrastructure projects, education and healthcare systems, and economic development initiatives that benefit both refugees and host communities. This approach helps to alleviate the immediate burden on host countries and lays the foundation for sustainable recovery and resilience.

Furthermore, international cooperation is essential in finding durable solutions for refugees, including voluntary repatriation, resettlement, and integration into host communities. Achieving these solutions requires a coordinated and comprehensive approach that respects the rights and dignity of refugees while considering the capacities and needs of host countries.

6 Conclusion

This chapter offers a comprehensive and forward-looking analysis of Lebanon's challenges and opportunities in the wake of the Syrian refugee crisis. Through a detailed examination of economic and social trajectories, strategic policy recommendations, and the emphasis on collaborative efforts and international cooperation, the chapter lays out a roadmap for Lebanon's recovery and growth. It underscores the importance of balancing immediate humanitarian needs with long-term economic planning and social integration, advocating for a multifaceted approach that encompasses fiscal reforms, infrastructure development, labour market adjustments, and enhanced social cohesion.

The chapter highlights the critical role of public-private partnerships, community-based initiatives, and international collaboration in addressing the complex challenges posed by the refugee crisis. It calls for strategic investments in Lebanon's economic resilience, the formalization of the labour market, and the integration of refugees into the economy as vital steps towards sustainable development. Furthermore, it emphasizes the necessity of promoting social cohesion and ensuring equitable access to services, laying the foundation for a stable and inclusive society.

The strategic recommendations presented in this chapter are not just a blueprint for Lebanon but also a call to action for the international community. The Syrian refugee crisis is a global challenge that requires a concerted and coordinated response. Lebanon's journey towards recovery and growth amidst this crisis can serve as a model for other nations facing similar challenges, highlighting the importance of resilience, innovation, and cooperation.

As Lebanon navigates the complexities of the refugee crisis and its aftermath, the insights and strategies outlined in this chapter provide valuable guidance. By embracing these recommendations, Lebanon can transform the challenges of today into the opportunities of tomorrow, ensuring a prosperous and stable future for all its residents, both Lebanese and refugees alike. This chapter is not only a reflection on what has been but also a vision of what could be, offering hope and direction for Lebanon as it moves forward.

References

Abi Ghanem, D. (2018). Energy, the city and everyday life: Living with power outages in post-war Lebanon. *Energy Research & Social Science, 36*, 36–43.

Akar, B. (2016). Dialogic pedagogies in educational settings for active citizenship, social cohesion and peacebuilding in Lebanon. *Education, Citizenship and Social Justice, 11*(1), 44–62.

Anouti, H., & Enna, A. (2023). Social instability in fragile state context: Exploring the dynamics between Syrian refugees and the Lebanese host community in Lebanon. *Contemporary Review of the Middle East, 10*(4), 364–385.

Archer, D., Almansi, F., DiGregorio, M., Roberts, D., Sharma, D., & Syam, D. (2014). Moving towards inclusive urban adaptation: Approaches to integrating community-based adaptation to climate change at city and national scale. *Climate and Development, 6*(4), 345–356.

Badra, N. (2022). Fiscal policy in times of high debt: Tale of Lebanon. *Middle East Development Journal, 14*(1), 32–42.

Baumann, H. (2021). The causes, nature, and effect of the current crisis of Lebanese capitalism. In *Power-sharing after civil war* (pp. 61–77). Routledge.

Blakemore, S. (2019). Faith-based diplomacy and interfaith dialogue. *Brill Research Perspectives in Diplomacy and Foreign Policy, 3*(2), 1–124.

Dimitrova, D. V., Ozdora-Aksak, E., & Connolly-Ahern, C. (2018). On the border of the Syrian refugee crisis: Views from two different cultural perspectives. *American Behavioral Scientist, 62*(4), 532–546.

Hamdar, B. C., Najjar, R., & Karameh, K. (2017). The Lebanese perception of the impact of small & medium enterprises (SMEs) on the national economy. *Journal of Economics and Public Finance, 3*(3), 330–342.

Kikano, F., Fauveaud, G., & Lizarralde, G. (2021). Policies of exclusion: The case of Syrian refugees in Lebanon. *Journal of Refugee Studies, 34*(1), 422–452.

Linders, D. (2013). Towards open development: Leveraging open data to improve the planning and coordination of international aid. *Government Information Quarterly, 30*(4), 426–434.

Nourpanah, S., & Poteet, M. (Eds.). (2016). *After the flight: The dynamics of refugee settlement and integration*. Cambridge Scholars Publishing.

Othman, A. (2022). The role of economic freedom, governance, and business environment in attracting foreign direct investment in the Arab region. *Journal of Economics and Business, 2*, 1–19.

Pandey, N., de Coninck, H., & Sagar, A. D. (2022). Beyond technology transfer: Innovation cooperation to advance sustainable development in developing countries. *Wiley Interdisciplinary Reviews: Energy and Environment, 11*(2), e422.

Sukkari, T. (2023). *Prioritization and framing of NGOs working with Syrian refugees in Lebanon*. Doctoral dissertation, Columbia University.

Villani, E., Greco, L., & Phillips, N. (2017). Understanding value creation in public-private partnerships: A comparative case study. *Journal of Management Studies, 54*(6), 876–905.

CHAPTER 10

Concluding Reflections: Lessons Learned and Global Implications of Lebanon's Experience with the Syrian Refugee Crisis

This book strives to provide original contributions by offering a detailed empirical examination of Lebanon's economic conditions and the extensive demographic analysis of Syrian refugees within Lebanon. By presenting data-driven insights and grounding them in a solid theoretical framework, this work aims to fill the gap in current literature regarding the micro and macro-economic impacts of large-scale refugee influxes in a host country. Furthermore, comparative analyses with other countries facing similar crises, such as Jordan and Turkey, are used to highlight unique challenges and innovative policy solutions that Lebanon might consider implementing.

The Syrian refugee crisis, one of the most significant humanitarian challenges of the twenty-first century, has left an indelible mark on the Middle East, particularly on Lebanon, a nation that has found itself at the epicentre of this unprecedented human displacement. Stemming from the outbreak of the Syrian Civil War in 2011, the crisis has propelled millions to flee their homes, seeking refuge from the violence and instability that have ravaged their country. Lebanon, with its geographic proximity and historical ties to Syria, has become a sanctuary for a vast number of these displaced individuals, significantly altering the socio-economic landscape of the host country. This influx, which has seen Lebanon host the highest number of refugees per capita in the world, has placed immense strain on the country's resources, infrastructure, and social fabric. The impact on

M. Zreik, *The Syrian Refugee Crisis and Lebanon's Economic Landscape*, https://doi.org/10.1007/978-3-031-68471-5_10

Lebanon has been multifaceted, affecting everything from the economy, public services, and labour markets to social cohesion and internal security. As this book draws to a close, it is essential to recapitulate the profound effects of the Syrian refugee crisis on Lebanon, not only to underscore the urgency and scale of the situation but also to set the stage for the concluding reflections. These reflections aim to synthesize the insights garnered throughout the book, offering a comprehensive overview of the challenges faced, the responses formulated, and the lessons learned, with an eye towards future implications for Lebanon, the region, and the global community at large in managing similar crises.

The Syrian refugee crisis has exerted profound economic pressures on Lebanon, manifesting in various challenging dimensions that have reshaped the country's economic landscape. One of the most significant impacts has been on the nation's gross domestic product (GDP), where the influx of refugees has contributed to both fiscal strains and shifts in economic output. The presence of a large refugee population has increased consumption demand but has also placed a considerable burden on public finances, due to the escalated need for public services and infrastructure. This situation is further complicated by Lebanon's pre-existing fiscal challenges, including a high public debt burden, making the economic ramifications of the refugee crisis particularly acute.

The labour market in Lebanon has also undergone significant changes, with an increase in the supply of labour leading to heightened competition for jobs, particularly in sectors where refugees can find employment without formal work permits. This has resulted in wage suppression and increased informality in the labour market, affecting both Lebanese citizens and Syrian refugees. The agricultural and construction sectors, for instance, have seen an influx of refugee labour, which, while filling labour shortages, has also sparked tensions over job competition and wage levels.

Inflationary pressures have emerged as another critical challenge, with the increased demand for goods and services, partly driven by the refugee population, leading to rising prices. This inflation has affected the cost of living for all residents, exacerbating economic hardship particularly among low-income families. Moreover, trade disruptions have occurred, as traditional trade routes and partnerships have been affected by the regional instability, impacting Lebanon's export and import dynamics. These economic impacts underscore the multifaceted challenges Lebanon faces due to the refugee crisis, highlighting the need for comprehensive strategies to mitigate these effects and foster economic resilience.

The social and political landscape in Lebanon has been significantly shaped by the Syrian refugee crisis, presenting both challenges and opportunities for the Lebanese host communities and the Syrian refugees themselves. The influx of over a million Syrian refugees into Lebanon has strained social fabrics and exacerbated pre-existing political tensions within a country already grappling with its complex sectarian makeup and fragile political equilibrium.

Socially, the refugee crisis has highlighted issues of integration and cohesion, with Lebanese communities facing an unprecedented challenge in accommodating such a large number of refugees. The presence of Syrian refugees has sometimes led to increased competition for limited resources, jobs, and public services, contributing to tensions and hostilities between the host communities and refugees. However, these challenges also present opportunities for fostering social solidarity and mutual understanding, as various non-governmental organizations and community groups have initiated programmes aimed at promoting dialogue and cooperation between Lebanese citizens and Syrian refugees.

Politically, the refugee crisis has had profound implications for Lebanon's governance and stability. The Lebanese political system, characterized by sectarian divisions and a delicate power-sharing arrangement, has been put under additional pressure, challenging the country's ability to manage the crisis effectively. The sheer number of refugees has also influenced Lebanese domestic politics, with political parties and movements adopting various stances on the crisis, ranging from calls for compassion and support to demands for repatriation.

Furthermore, the prolonged presence of Syrian refugees in Lebanon raises significant questions about integration and long-term coexistence. Issues such as legal status, access to employment, and education for refugees are critical for ensuring that the refugees can live with dignity and contribute positively to their host communities. Addressing these issues requires nuanced and empathetic policy responses that consider the socio-political realities of Lebanon and the well-being of both Lebanese citizens and Syrian refugees.

The international community's response to the Syrian refugee crisis in Lebanon has been multifaceted, involving aid, diplomatic support, and economic assistance. This response has been coordinated through various international organizations, donor countries, and NGOs, aiming to alleviate the humanitarian plight of Syrian refugees and support the Lebanese host community.

Aid has primarily been in the form of humanitarian assistance, including food, shelter, medical care, and education services for refugees. Significant funding has also been directed towards infrastructure and public services in Lebanon to help the country cope with the increased demand. Diplomatic efforts have focused on seeking a political resolution to the Syrian conflict and encouraging international burden-sharing to prevent Lebanon and other host countries from shouldering the crisis alone.

Economic assistance has included direct financial support to the Lebanese government and investment in projects aimed at stimulating economic growth and creating job opportunities for both Lebanese citizens and Syrian refugees. This includes initiatives to improve the country's public infrastructure, water supply, and waste management systems, which have been under severe strain.

Despite these efforts, the international response has faced criticism for its limitations. The aid provided has often been deemed insufficient to meet the vast needs, and funding shortfalls have frequently resulted in cuts to essential services. Economic assistance has not fully addressed the structural challenges of the Lebanese economy, which has been further exacerbated by the crisis. Furthermore, diplomatic efforts have yet to yield a lasting solution to the Syrian conflict, prolonging the displacement issue.

The strategic recommendations for Lebanon and the international community to navigate the complexities of the Syrian refugee crisis emphasize a holistic approach, integrating economic, social, and political strategies to forge sustainable solutions. To stabilize and grow Lebanon's economy, it's imperative to undertake fiscal and economic reforms that not only enhance stability but also attract investments. These efforts should be bolstered by international financial aid and investments in infrastructure projects, which are instrumental in generating employment opportunities for both Lebanese citizens and Syrian refugees, thereby fostering economic development.

The integration of Syrian refugees into the labour market is a critical aspect of these recommendations. By facilitating the legal employment of refugees, Lebanon can reduce their dependency on humanitarian aid, allowing them to contribute to the host country's economy. This approach must be carefully balanced to ensure it also meets the employment needs and rights of the Lebanese population, promoting harmony and mutual benefit.

Education and social integration initiatives are paramount for the long-term integration of refugees into Lebanese society. Investing in education for refugee children and adults lays the foundation for their future success and integration. Furthermore, programmes designed to promote social cohesion between refugees and host communities can play a vital role in alleviating tensions and fostering a sense of mutual understanding and respect.

To effectively manage the challenges posed by the refugee crisis, Lebanon must also embark on policy and governance reforms. Strengthening governance and enhancing public services are essential steps towards a more effective management of the refugee presence. This includes establishing transparent and accountable mechanisms for the distribution of aid and the development of infrastructure.

The role of the international community cannot be overstated. Continued financial and diplomatic support is crucial, ensuring that assistance is both responsive and adaptive to the evolving needs of Lebanon and its refugee population. A coordinated international approach, involving host countries, donor states, and international organizations, is essential for sharing responsibilities and promoting regional stability. While immediate aid and support are necessary, the pursuit of long-term solutions for Syrian refugees, including voluntary repatriation, resettlement, and integration, should proceed in parallel.

These efforts must respect the rights and dignity of refugees, aiming to provide them with stable and secure futures. Through the implementation of these comprehensive strategies, Lebanon and the international community can address the immediate challenges of the refugee crisis while laying the groundwork for a stable and prosperous future for both Lebanese and Syrian populations.

Lebanon's experience with the Syrian refugee crisis provides critical insights into how a nation can adapt to substantial economic shocks, offering lessons in resilience and the need for agile economic policy adjustments. The influx of over a million Syrian refugees into Lebanon, a country with a pre-crisis population of just over four million, created unprecedented economic pressures. Yet, it also catalysed a series of adaptations and policy responses that underscore the potential for resilience in the face of such challenges.

The initial economic shock was multifaceted, impacting labour markets, public services, and infrastructure. Lebanon's already fragile economy, burdened by high debt levels and political instability, faced further strain as the demand for housing, education, healthcare, and employment surged. This situation could have led to an economic breakdown, but instead, it prompted a series of adaptations that offer valuable lessons.

First, Lebanon's response highlighted the importance of flexibility in economic policy. Recognizing the strain on public services, the Lebanese government, with the support of international donors, embarked on initiatives aimed at expanding and strengthening infrastructure and public services. This not only addressed immediate needs but also laid the groundwork for longer-term improvements in the country's economic capacity.

Second, the crisis underscored the need for inclusive labour market policies. With the influx of Syrian refugees, competition for jobs intensified, initially leading to tensions and a rise in unemployment among the Lebanese population. In response, Lebanon explored policies that balanced the need to protect the livelihoods of its citizens with the reality of the refugee presence. This included initiatives to formalize the status of Syrian workers, integrate them into the economy, and thus mitigate the impact on wages and employment for Lebanese workers.

Furthermore, Lebanon's adaptation to the economic shock brought about by the refugee crisis demonstrated the critical role of international cooperation and aid. Financial assistance, investment in infrastructure, and support for public services from the international community were pivotal in stabilizing the Lebanese economy. This cooperation highlighted the interdependence of nations in addressing global challenges and the importance of international solidarity in crisis response.

The crisis offered lessons in the resilience of the private sector. Faced with new challenges, many Lebanese businesses adapted by exploring new markets, diversifying their services, and employing innovative solutions to meet the changing needs of their customer base, which now included a significant number of refugees.

The Syrian refugee crisis, one of the largest displacement events in recent history, has significantly impacted Lebanon, testing the social fabric of the country. The presence of Syrian refugees has introduced new dynamics into Lebanese communities, presenting both challenges and opportunities for social integration and cohesion. Strategies to foster a harmonious coexistence have ranged from community-based initiatives to policy interventions, reflecting a multifaceted approach to building a cohesive society.

Community-based initiatives have been at the forefront of promoting social integration. These grassroots efforts often focus on creating shared spaces and opportunities for Lebanese and Syrian individuals to come together, emphasizing commonalities rather than differences. For example, joint educational programmes and vocational training sessions have been effective in bridging divides, allowing participants to focus on mutual goals and shared challenges. Additionally, cultural events celebrating both Lebanese and Syrian heritage have served as a powerful tool for fostering mutual understanding and respect. These initiatives not only facilitate personal connections but also help dispel myths and stereotypes, laying the groundwork for deeper social cohesion.

Policy interventions have also played a crucial role in promoting social integration. The Lebanese government, with support from international organizations, has sought to implement policies aimed at ensuring equal access to services and economic opportunities for refugees and host communities alike. This includes efforts to integrate Syrian children into the public education system, providing a foundation for long-term social cohesion through shared learning experiences. Moreover, policies designed to facilitate legal residency and work permits for Syrian refugees have been critical in reducing vulnerabilities and promoting economic independence, which, in turn, supports social integration by addressing some of the root causes of tension between communities.

However, fostering social integration and cohesion in such a complex context is not without its challenges. Economic strain, competition for resources, and political sensitivities have sometimes hindered progress. Addressing these challenges requires a sustained commitment to inclusivity, dialogue, and mutual respect. It also necessitates a recognition of the importance of psychological and social support for both refugees and host communities, who have faced significant stressors and traumas.

Efforts to foster social integration and cohesion in Lebanon highlight the importance of a comprehensive approach that combines community engagement with supportive policies. Such efforts are crucial not only for the well-being of Syrian refugees but also for the stability and prosperity of Lebanese host communities. By focusing on shared goals, fostering dialogue, and addressing economic and social disparities, Lebanon can continue to build a more cohesive and harmonious society. This experience offers valuable lessons for other countries facing similar challenges, underscoring the potential of community resilience and the transformative power of inclusive policies in overcoming the divides wrought by displacement and conflict.

The Syrian refugee crisis and its impact on Lebanon underscore the critical importance of international solidarity and cooperation in managing large-scale refugee situations. Lebanon's experience offers valuable lessons for the global community, emphasizing the need for a coordinated, comprehensive approach to crisis management that transcends national borders.

Lebanon's handling of the refugee influx demonstrates the limitations of any single country's capacity to absorb and support a large number of refugees without substantial international assistance. Despite Lebanon's considerable efforts to accommodate Syrian refugees, the sheer scale of the crisis has strained its economic, social, and infrastructural capacities. This situation highlights the necessity of international solidarity—not as a matter of charity but as a fundamental aspect of shared global responsibility. The international community's support through financial aid, infrastructure development projects, and technical assistance has been indispensable in mitigating the impact of the crisis on both refugees and host communities.

Moreover, Lebanon's experience has revealed the importance of cooperation among nations and international organizations in crafting and implementing effective response strategies. The collaboration between the Lebanese government, the United Nations, non-governmental organizations, and donor countries has facilitated the delivery of humanitarian aid, the provision of education and healthcare services, and the implementation of economic development projects. This cooperative approach should serve as a model for future crisis responses, emphasizing the need for a unified strategy that addresses immediate humanitarian needs while also considering long-term development goals.

The crisis has also illustrated the significance of burden-sharing among countries. Lebanon, a small country with its own complex socio-political challenges, has hosted a disproportionately large number of refugees. This situation calls for a more equitable distribution of responsibilities, with other nations stepping up to provide refuge, financial support, and resettlement options. International solidarity in crisis management should manifest in tangible actions that alleviate the burden on frontline countries.

Lebanon's experience emphasizes the need for sustainable solutions that go beyond temporary relief efforts. The protracted nature of the Syrian conflict has made it clear that refugee crises require long-term planning and investment in durable solutions, including support for voluntary repatriation, local integration, and resettlement in third countries. These efforts must be underpinned by a commitment to uphold the rights and dignity of refugees, ensuring their access to education, employment, and social services.

Improving the effectiveness and coordination of aid in response to humanitarian crises requires a nuanced understanding of the complexities involved in bringing together international actors, NGOs, and host governments. The experience of Lebanon, which has found itself at the forefront of the Syrian refugee crisis, offers valuable insights into how aid effectiveness and coordination can be enhanced to better serve the needs of affected populations.

A key factor in improving aid delivery is the establishment of clear coordination mechanisms. The need for a centralized platform or oversight body becomes apparent when considering the myriad of actors involved in crisis response efforts. Such a mechanism can streamline the distribution of resources, prevent the duplication of efforts, and ensure that assistance reaches those in greatest need. In Lebanon, the collaborative efforts between United Nations agencies, international NGOs, and the Lebanese government have underscored the potential benefits of a coordinated approach. However, challenges remain in fully integrating and aligning the diverse objectives and operational modalities of these actors.

Another crucial aspect is the need for comprehensive and ongoing assessments of the needs of affected populations. These assessments should inform the planning and implementation of aid programmes, ensuring they are responsive to the evolving situation on the ground. In the context of Lebanon, the dynamic nature of the refugee crisis, with fluctuating numbers and changing needs, has highlighted the importance of adaptable and flexible aid strategies. By basing aid efforts on accurate and current information, stakeholders can improve the relevance and impact of their interventions.

Effective communication and information sharing among all parties involved in aid delivery are also vital. This includes not only international actors and NGOs but also local communities and the refugees themselves. Engaging with local stakeholders and beneficiaries ensures that aid programmes are culturally sensitive and aligned with the actual needs of the population. Moreover, it fosters a sense of ownership and empowerment among those directly affected by the crisis.

The importance of building local capacities cannot be overstated. Supporting local governments and community organizations enhances the sustainability of aid efforts and strengthens resilience against future crises. In Lebanon, empowering local entities has been instrumental in sustaining response efforts over the long term. This approach not only bolsters immediate aid delivery but also contributes to the development of robust systems capable of managing ongoing and future challenges.

Developing robust policy frameworks for refugee integration and host community resilience in crisis situations is a critical global imperative. The experiences of countries like Lebanon, hosting a significant number of Syrian refugees, offer valuable lessons on formulating policies that not only support refugee integration but also bolster the resilience of host communities. Such frameworks must be multidimensional, addressing immediate humanitarian needs while laying the groundwork for long-term social and economic inclusion.

A key recommendation is the establishment of legal pathways for refugees that clarify their status and rights within host countries. These pathways should include the right to work, access to education, and healthcare services, which are fundamental for enabling refugees to live with dignity and contribute to their host societies. Legal recognition is the first step towards integration, providing refugees with a sense of security and belonging, and reducing vulnerabilities to exploitation and marginalization.

Equally important is the investment in social infrastructure to accommodate the needs of both refugees and host communities. This involves scaling up public services such as education, healthcare, and housing to prevent overburdening existing facilities. Policies should promote equitable access to these services, ensuring that refugees and host communities benefit from enhanced capacities. For instance, educational programmes must be inclusive, providing language training and psychosocial support to refugee children, thereby facilitating their integration into the national schooling system.

Economic inclusion strategies are also vital. Governments, with the support of international organizations and the private sector, should create employment opportunities for refugees that also benefit local economies. This can be achieved through vocational training programmes, entrepreneurship schemes, and incentives for businesses that employ both locals and refugees. Such initiatives not only aid in the economic integration of refugees but also contribute to the overall development of host communities.

Furthermore, fostering social cohesion and intercommunity dialogue is crucial. Policies should encourage interactions and mutual understanding between refugees and host communities, dispelling myths and building bridges. Community centres, cultural events, and joint community projects can play a significant role in promoting harmonious coexistence.

International cooperation and burden-sharing are indispensable. Robust policy frameworks for refugee integration require sustained financial and technical support from the international community. This support should be aligned with the specific needs and capacities of host countries, ensuring that policies are not only ambitious but also feasible and sustainable.

For Lebanon to navigate its complex socio-economic challenges, exacerbated by the Syrian refugee crisis, it must adopt strategies aimed at strengthening its economic and social structures to ensure long-term resilience and growth. Central to this endeavour is the need for comprehensive economic reforms. Lebanon should prioritize fiscal stability, tackling its burgeoning debt through policy measures that encourage fiscal discipline, diversify revenue sources, and rationalize public spending. Implementing structural reforms in key sectors such as energy, telecommunications, and public transportation can attract foreign investment, improve competitiveness, and stimulate economic growth.

Moreover, Lebanon must invest in its human capital. Enhancing the quality of education and vocational training can equip both the Lebanese youth and Syrian refugees with the skills needed for the modern labour market. Such initiatives not only improve individual livelihoods but also contribute to the country's overall economic development. Additionally, integrating refugees into the economy through legal work opportunities can alleviate the burden on public services by reducing dependency on aid and enabling refugees to contribute to the host economy.

Social cohesion is another pillar requiring reinforcement. Lebanon should foster an inclusive society that embraces diversity and mitigates tensions between different communities. This involves promoting dialogue and understanding, addressing disparities, and ensuring equitable access to services for all residents, irrespective of their nationality or status. Strengthening social safety nets and providing support for vulnerable populations, including both Lebanese citizens and Syrian refugees, are crucial steps towards building a resilient society.

The international community plays a pivotal role in supporting nations like Lebanon, which are disproportionately affected by refugee crises. Enhancing international cooperation necessitates a commitment to shared responsibility, recognizing that the challenges posed by such crises transcend national borders and require a collective response. Developed countries should increase their financial contributions to humanitarian and development aid, ensuring that funds are allocated efficiently and transparently to meet the most pressing needs of refugees and host communities.

Moreover, international support should not only address immediate humanitarian needs but also focus on sustainable development initiatives that bolster the host country's infrastructure, economy, and public services. This includes investing in projects that enhance water supply, sanitation, healthcare, education, and renewable energy sources. Such investments not only improve the quality of life for both refugees and host communities but also contribute to environmental sustainability and economic resilience.

Encouraging public-private partnerships can mobilize additional resources and expertise for development projects. The private sector can play a crucial role in creating job opportunities, advancing technological solutions, and fostering innovation. Additionally, resettlement programmes and legal migration pathways should be expanded, offering refugees more durable solutions while alleviating the pressure on host countries.

Addressing refugee crises in the twenty-first century demands innovative approaches that leverage technology, foster public-private partnerships, and employ multilateral diplomacy. Technology can revolutionize how aid is delivered and how refugees access services. Digital platforms can streamline registration processes, enhance the coordination of aid distribution, and provide refugees with critical information on legal assistance, healthcare, and education. Mobile banking and cash transfer programmes can offer refugees a secure means to receive financial support, empowering them with choice and dignity in meeting their needs.

Public-private partnerships represent a powerful tool for addressing the multifaceted challenges of refugee crises. The private sector's agility, resources, and innovation can complement the efforts of governments and NGOs, whether through creating employment opportunities for refugees, investing in infrastructure projects, or providing technological solutions to improve aid delivery and integration efforts. Encouraging entrepreneurship among refugees not only facilitates their economic integration but also contributes to the host country's economic dynamism.

Furthermore, multilateral diplomacy is essential in seeking sustainable solutions to the root causes of refugee movements. The international community must work together to address conflicts, human rights abuses, and governance issues that drive people to flee their homes. Diplomatic efforts should aim at peacebuilding, supporting democratic transitions, and promoting human rights protections. Engaging in dialogue with all stakeholders, including refugees themselves, is crucial in crafting policies that are both effective and respectful of refugees' rights and dignity.

Index

M. Zreik, *The Syrian Refugee Crisis and Lebanon's Economic Landscape*, https://doi.org/10.1007/978-3-031-68471-5

S

T

U

V

W

The manufacturer's authorised representative in the EU is Springer Nature Customer Service Centre GmbH, Europaplatz 3, 69115 Heidelberg, Germany. If you have any concerns regarding our products, please contact ProductSafety@springernature.com

Printed and bound by CPI Group (UK) Ltd, Croydon, CR0 4YY

01/10/2026

02225967-0001